WINNING
AT
MATH

Your Guide to Learning Mathematics Through Successful Study Skills

SEVENTH EDITION
With New Content

Paul D. Nolting, Ph.D.
Learning Specialist

Academic Success Press, Inc.
FLORIDA

This book is dedicated to my son, Eric, to my wife, Kim, and to the memory of my good friend Bill Thomas. It is also dedicated to the thousands of students who are having difficulty learning mathematics and the instructors who are teaching them.

Winning at Math:
Your Guide to Learning Mathematics
Through Successful Study Skills
(Seventh Edition)
by Paul D. Nolting, Ph.D.
Seventh Edition with New Content, 2018
Copyright © 2020 by Paul D. Nolting, Ph.D.
978-0-940287-73-0
Published by Academic Success Press, Inc.
Editor: Daniel Crown
Assistant Editor: Kimberly Nolting
Photo Credits: Unless otherwise noted, all photos and clipart are reproduced
with the permission of
Fotosearch.com and ClipArt.com.

Printed in the United States of America.

Contents

Preface

College students have a complicated relationship with mathematics. Some love math's ironclad logic and challenges. Others dislike the subject and have difficulty learning its concepts. While students are allowed to feel any way they want about math, the necessity of the subject is beyond debate. Students must pass math to graduate college.

Too many students are intimidated by math because they have a poor math background, have test anxiety, or they are returning to school for the first time in many years. These students understand that, like it or not, thriving in their math courses leads to more career options and better paying jobs. For this reason, students need assistance to succeed in math. Tutoring is just one part of the equation. Students need tips and procedures that are easy to implement: math-specific study skills, organizational skills, and test-taking strategies for traditional and online courses.

Winning at Math — Seventh Edition is the only study skills book with math-specific study strategies, which offers statistical evidence on how to improve math learning and grades. The math study skills, anxiety reduction techniques, and test-taking procedures provided in *Winning at Math — Seventh Edition* are based on learning specialist Dr. Paul D. Nolting's 30 years of research with colleges and universities. The techniques in the text are equally effective with first-time students, repeating students, students taking developmental math, and students taking credited courses. Evidence also suggests that the book leads to improvement in other non-math courses as well.

Learning math requires a different set of learning skills, testing skills, and anxiety reduction techniques than those used in other courses. That's why general study skills courses or freshman seminar courses are not typically successful in improving math grades. For this reason, many students make "A's" and "B's" in all other courses but have difficulty passing math. By using the suggested study procedures in *Winning at Math — Seventh Edition*, you can improve your math grades by using these strategies and developing an individualized math success plan.

We have revised this edition of *Winning at Math* for faster and more efficient use. To start with, we've reduced the page count by more than a third. This doesn't mean we've weakened the book in any way. It still contains the essential math study skills from the original text. It's just that we've updated much of the text to better reflect the modern classroom. This includes specific new skills for several modern math class models, as well as new test-anxiety reduction, self-motivation, note-taking, and tutoring techniques.

The book emphasize success in all types of designs, including co-requisite and computer-based learning courses. Some designs require students to learn quickly and independently. They also require new and specific study-skills, which are described in detail throughout this text.

Finally, we have also added a Checklist for Knowledge and Behaviors to the end of each chapter. These checklists are designed to make sure students understand key points and key study behaviors. Each chapter also includes additional activities, which are new to this edition. As always, this edition of *Winning at Math* includes Web-based support in the form of the revised Math Study Skills Evaluation. The first chapter now focuses on student motivation, math self-efficacy, and the money in math.

What's New in the 7th Edition?

New Topics Include

- Self-learning
- Mindfulness and learning
- How to improve math self-efficacy
- Mindsets concepts
- Taking notes with technology
- Math technology/apps
- Making a resource plan
- How to work effectively with tutors and classmates
- Attitudes towards tests
- Mindfulness for reducing anxiety
- Stages of memory chart
- Student scenarios
- Appendix D - Classroom Group Learning Activities
- Checklists for Knowledge
- Checklists for Behaviors
- Updated references throughout
- Updated terminology and terms
- Rewrite of chapters to make them more personable to students

Expanded Topics Include

- Reshaping your attitudes toward math and how math pays Off
- Obstacles to success
- How to create a weekly study plan
- How to manage work and study schedule
- Distance learning, computer-based learning and online homework
- How to use learning resources centers and distance learning resources
- How to recall what you have learned
- Stages of memory
- New memory chart
- Learning preferences
- Creating and implementng a plan
- Appendix A - apps, websites and search engines for academic support

Winning at Math helps you become successful in mathematics by teaching you how to study on your own or as a part of a classroom or lab. This is true whether you are enrolled in a traditional math course, a modular course, a co-requisite course, or a computer-based learning course. *Winning at Math* helps students who struggle with math, but also helps successful students to become more efficient learners. It helps these students improve grades and remember information longer with less effort.

Also, by going to www.AcademicSuccess.com and clicking on the "Winning at Math Student Resources" button — using "Wam" as the username and "Student" as the password — you can access the Math Study Skills Evaluation — 7th-edition, How to Reduce Test Anxiety audio file, online homework, check lists, and other resources to improve math learning.

How Learning Math is Different and How To Take Control of Your Learning

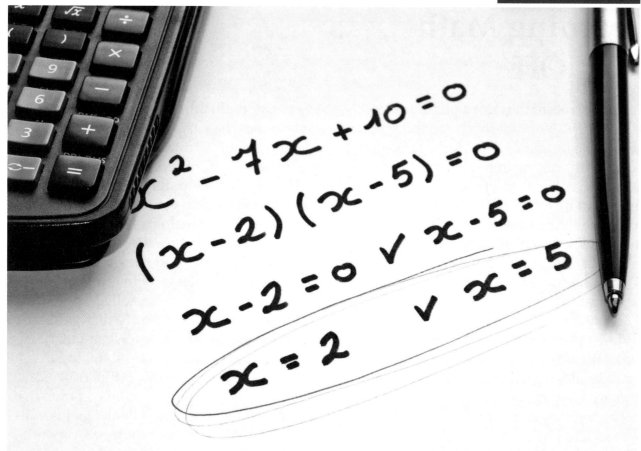

In Chapter 1
You will learn these concepts:

✓ How attitudes toward math affect learning

✓ How assessing math study skills improves study behaviors

✓ How studying math differs from studying other subjects

✓ How to take control of math and motivate yourself

✓ How to communicate with your professor

Reshaping Your Attitude Toward Math and How Learning Math Pays Off

It's no secret math is not a popular subject these days. Not that this is anything new. From the moment man first began counting on his fingers, math has been the ultimate love or hate subject—even among the greatest minds in history. For every math-centric thinker like Pythagoras or Isaac Newton, there's at least one contrarian like Augustine of Hippo, a 5th-century philosopher who once claimed that mathematicians had made a covenant with the devil "to darken the spirit" and "confine man in the bonds of Hell."

While most modern math students may not take their disdain for the subject quite as far as jolly-old-Augustine, the fact remains that many view math differently than they do other courses. According to a recent poll conducted by Amplicate.com, nearly 86 percent of high school students claim to "hate" algebra. The same data shows that geometry is by far the most reviled subject for students under the age of eighteen. Recent academic inquiries reinforce this data. In 2017, researchers found that most college students see math as a major roadblock to their success (Acee, et.al, 2017). However, some students have a positive attitude towards math, and this text can help maintain that attitude when taking more difficult courses.

If you are a college student, and the negative description rings a bell, you need to remember two things. First, there's nothing wrong with disliking math. Second, plenty of students who hate math pass it anyway.

A negative math attitude is only dangerous if it becomes the basis for bad behavior. If a negative math attitude leads to poor class attendance, poor concentration and poor study skills, however, then you have more than a bad attitude—you have a problem.

The key to combating a bad math attitude is to develop persistence. Persistence, perhaps more than any other behavior, is absolutely crucial to success, not only in terms of passing math and graduating from college, but also in determining one's ability to thrive in the outside world. As former U.S. President Calvin Coolidge once wrote: "Nothing in this world can take the place of persistence. Talent will not; nothing is more common than unsuccessful people with talent. Genius will not; unrewarded genius is almost a proverb. Persistence and determination alone are omnipotent. The slogan 'press on' has solved and always will solve the problems of the human race."

Even the most capable student cannot succeed in college without the ability to learn from failure. In the same way, those who struggle with math are just as capable of success, so long as they "press on" through their problems. By coupling a positive attitude with study and test-taking skills, you are entirely capable of rising above any challenges, big or small. If you see math as one of these challenges, that's perfectly okay. Don't give up. Remember, the harder the challenge, the greater the reward.

Opinions about mathematics are all over the map. Even the greatest minds this planet has ever known can't come to a consensus.

Mathematics is like checkers in being suitable for the young, not too difficult, amusing, and without peril to the state.
—Plato

Do not worry about your difficulties in Mathematics. I can assure you mine are still greater.
— Albert Einstein

God used beautiful mathematics in creating the world.
—Paul Dirac

Mathematicians have made a covenant with the devil to darken the spirit and to confine man in the bonds of hell.
—Augustine of Hippo

What do you think about math?

How Learning Math Pays Off

Now that we've learned how math is different, how to end negative self-talk, and the importance of persistence, what do we want to gain from learning math?

Another way to ask this question is, "What are your reasons for attending college?" Are you going to college to better yourself? Are you going to college to obtain the career you want? Are you going to college to make more money? I ask these questions to many students who are taking math, and what do you think is the most popular response? You're right! Most students say they are going to college to make more money. Students also indicate they want to like their careers and make enough money to live a better life. It does not matter if these students are going for an Associate of Science degree, an Associate of Arts degree or a Baccalaureate degree. Their goals are to graduate in the shortest amount of time and to obtain a high paying career.

Students also often indicate they want their career to be secure so they will not have to keep switching employment or have to be retrained. This is especially true of men and women who are returning to college to obtain better careers to support their families. Being clear on your college goal is a way to motivate your college success. So does taking math courses mean you can obtain a higher paying career, have more career options, and put together a competitive resume? YES!

Associate of Science degrees are usually two-year degrees once you have been admitted to a program or once you have completed the prerequisite courses. Four of the five highest paying jobs a student can get with an Associate's degree (dental hygienists, diagnostic medical sonographers, registered nurses, radiation therapists) require college algebra or statistics. The national salary for these careers range from about $60,000 to $80,000 with registered nurse being the lowest and computer occupations being the highest paid careers. Four of the five lowest paying jobs (veterinary technician, medical records

technician, physical therapist assistant, and occupational therapist assistant) require mathematics courses below college algebra and statistics. The national salary for these careers range from about $25,000 to about $55,000 with veterinary technician being the lowest and radiological technologist being the highest paid position. Based on this information, if you want the most job selections and highest paying career, then passing more mathematics courses is your ticket to success.

Students who are going for a Baccalaureate degree either obtain an Associate of Arts degree at a community/junior college or are already attending a university. In most cases, these students will make more money than students with Associate in Science degrees. One way to look at these majors is to plot the graph by using salaries and the increasing amounts of math courses. The graph on page 12 demonstrates the 20 top careers with the best pay, fastest growth, and the most openings for the 21st century. It also shows national annual salary per year (Farr and Ludden, Best Jobs of the 21st Century, 2013).

Look at the pattern. All five highest paying jobs (software developer, network administrator, construction manager, engineer, computer systems analysts) require business calculus or higher. In fact, all nine careers that have salaries around $50,000 a year require business calculus or a higher math course. Four of the five lowest paying jobs (physical therapy assistant, paralegal assistant, veterinary technology assistant) require mathematics courses below college algebra and statistics.

By now, using your excellent number sense, you have figured it out. The more math courses you take, the higher paying career you will get! Learning mathematics is the key to finding success in your personal, academic, and professional lives.

Now that you know that taking more mathematics means more career choices and better pay, how can you accomplish this goal? Effective learning strategies for successful math study skills leads to more math success. Math success helps you graduate and allows you to select majors in areas that lead to high paying jobs and more job security.

Obstacles to Success

Sometimes, self-talk and statements by others may block your motivation to become successful in your math course. Don't get in the habit of saying, "When will I ever use this math?" or "Why do I have to take this math course because I will not use it in my job?"

These statements may make you feel better when you are not successful in a math course; however, they also lead to poor motivation and less studying. The real questions are: "Do I need this math course to graduate?" or "Do I need this math course as a prerequisite to enter my major?"

For example, if you are a business major, in most cases you'll need applied calculus to be accepted to the college of business. Being successful in applied calculus is your "ticket" to your business major and making that million dollars.

You must also void negative statements from other students about math. Some of your classmates may get into a discussion about their struggles with math. They start complaining about math course or instructors, wanting you to join in. It makes them feel

Don't let obstacles get in the way of your success in math. Stay persistent and obtain the career you've always wanted.

better if you confirm their feelings. WATCH OUT! This is a psychological trap. Negative thoughts cause lower effort and even failure.

Find students who are positive about math or see passing math as a way to become successful in college and life. If you already like math, then help others to have a positive math attitude.

Finally, some students must take developmental math courses in order to be ready to take required math courses. If this happens to you, don't be discouraged! I have personally worked with hundreds of students who began in the lowest developmental math courses and now have their business, engineering, computer science, or economics degrees. Thousands of students have finished their developmental math courses and have completed college algebra or calculus and are now in their careers. Remember, this effort and persistence is worth your time. More math equals more money!

Best Jobs Requiring a Bachelor's Degree

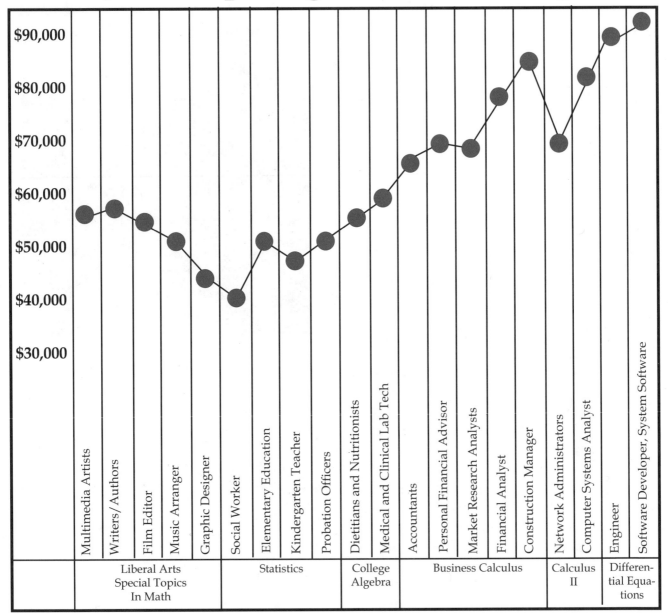

Source: *Best Jobs for the 21st Century*, Sixth Edition © JIST Works 2012
Graph: © Academic Success Press Inc. 2013

Activity 1.1 What type of career do you want?

Choosing a career is tricky. Sometimes our interests and our desire for a highly compensated career do not match up. This means that many students who do not like math will still have to take numerous math courses to obtain their degree. Fill out the form below to find out just how much math you will need to take to graduate and start your career.

1. What type of career do you want to have when you finish college? If undecided, then write down the general field you might want to go into (humanities, science, business, etc.)

2. How much money do you want to make in your career? Write the total in the space below.

3. Look at the chart on the previous page. Do you see your career? If so, see if your career goals match the amount of money you want to make. After you have done this, write down the math courses you will need to take to finish your degree.

4. If your chosen career is not on the chart, either use the Internet to look up the information you need, or visit your career counselor or Career Center. Follow the same procedure as the question above.

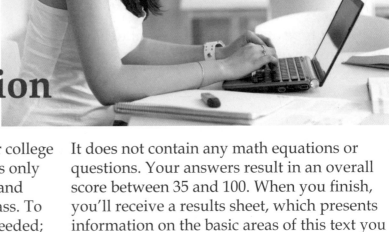

Taking the Math Study Skills Evaluation

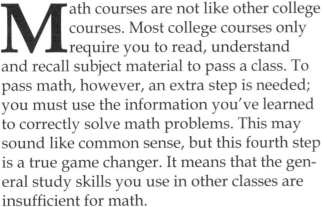

Math courses are not like other college courses. Most college courses only require you to read, understand and recall subject material to pass a class. To pass math, however, an extra step is needed; you must use the information you've learned to correctly solve math problems. This may sound like common sense, but this fourth step is a true game changer. It means that the general study skills you use in other classes are insufficient for math.

To get better grades in math, you need to learn math-specific study skills. These skills help you build confidence and achieve better grades. They also help you reduce your math-based anxiety—especially during your first college math course. This book not only covers these study skills, but also allows you to custom build your own study plan by addressing your unique strengths and challenges.

Before learning what study strategies work best for you, however, it's first important to take the Math Study Skills Evaluation—7th Edition. To access the MSSE—7 visit AcademicSuccess.com— Student Resources and enter "WAM" for the username and "Student" for the password. This program determines what you know about how to study for math and helps you determine what material in this book will help you improve success in your math course. The MSSE—7 involves answering a series of questions about your basic study behaviors.

It does not contain any math equations or questions. Your answers result in an overall score between 35 and 100. When you finish, you'll receive a results sheet, which presents information on the basic areas of this text you already understand, as well as those areas on which you can improve.

Your overall score and accompanying advice will look something like this:

Sally College, the overall result of your evaluation is a score of 47. A score of 70 and below means you need to improve your math study skills and this could be the main reason you are having difficulty learning math.

You will also receive specific results on one of many subjects:

You have a score of 48 in Memory and Learning, which measures your understanding of learning preferences and the learning process, as well as your ability to develop a useful learning plan. You need to read and study chapter 6.

If your results seem low, don't worry! This low score may explain your poor math grades, and you now know exactly what you need to work on! If you've spent your entire academic life using inefficient study skills, this is likely the source of your problems with math. The skills you'll read about in this book will directly address this.

Activity 1.2   Math Study Skills Evaluation Results

Now, it's time to take the Math Study Skills Evaluation! To do so, visit the following website: www.academicsuccess.com. Click on "Student Resources" and enter the following information: username: WAM
password: Student

Student Name_____   Date_____

Advisor Name_____   Email_____

Overall result_____
A score of 79 and below means you need to improve your math study skills, and this could be the main reason you have had difficulty learning math.

Study Effectively_____, which measures how well you understand that studying for math differs from studying for other subjects. It also measures your effective use of study goals, reading/homework systems, study tools, and motivation. The reference chapter is Chapter One.

Memory and Learning_____, which measures what you know about learning styles, the learning process, as well as developing a learning plan and memory strategies. The reference chapter is Chapter Six.

Reading and Homework_____, which measures how well you understand a course's syllabus and what you know about developing reading and homework strategies to improve math learning. The reference chapters are Chapter Three and Chapter Four.

Classroom Learning_____, which measures the ability to develop listening strategies, note-taking systems as well as the ability to ask questions. The reference chapter is Chapter Two.

Test Anxiety and Test Taking_____, which measures how well you understand the effects of test anxiety, how to reduce test anxiety, how to take tests and how to analyze test results. The reference chapters are Chapter Five.

Based on your scores and a discussion with your advisor, list from most important to least important the order of the chapters in this text you most need to read:

Chapter___,
Chapter___,
Chapter___,
Chapter___,
Chapter___,
Chapter___,

I will complete reading these chapters by this date: _____

How Learning Math Is Different

To learn and thrive in your math courses, it's important to understand the basic elements of the learning process. Math courses require you to do four things:

1. Understand material
2. Process material
3. Apply what you've learned to correctly solve a problem
4. Remember everything you've already learned to learn new material

These four tasks help you master the math you must learn. If you do not complete one of the tasks, you will not complete the others. In other words, in order to successfully complete math problems, you must actively engage with the topics you are studying in real time. This is not true in most other courses.

Example: Political science courses require you to learn about politics and public service, but your instructor will not make you run for governor to pass the course. In math, however, you must be able to correctly solve problems. When you learn about factoring techniques, for example, you must solve numerous factoring problems in order to pass a test.

Math as Sequential Learning

Another way math differs from other subjects is that it uses a sequential learning pattern. The material you learn on one day is used the next day and the next day and so forth.

Example: Learning math is like building a house. Houses are built from the ground up: you build the foundation first, then the walls, then the roof. Math is the same way. It must be learned in a specific order. You cannot learn complex problems without first learning simple ones.

Unlike other subjects, you cannot forget important material after a math test. Each chapter in a math book is a foundation block for the next. All building blocks must be included to successfully learn math. This building-block approach to learning math is the reason why it's difficult to catch up when you get behind. You can't skip information in one chapter to hurry up and get caught up in the next. To succeed in math, each previous chapter has to be completely understood before continuing to the next chapter.

Sequential learning also affects studying for math tests. If you understand Chapter 1 and 2 but do not understand Chapter 3, you will not understand Chapter 4. When test time approaches, you end up trying to teach yourself too many concepts while studying for the test when you should be reviewing and practicing. This makes it likely your results won't represent the best you can do.

Now that you understand how learning math is a building experience, what should you do if you've already fallen behind?

1. *Don't get anxious.* Stay calm.

2. *If your college* has a diagnostic math inventory in the tutoring center or math lab, take it to see what math concepts you've forgotten, and ask your instructor where you can go to relearn these math concepts.

3. *Take the time* to follow through. Many students give up too easily, or they think they'll catch up a little at a time. The energy you put into your class at the beginning of the session will be more productive than energy put into class at the end of the session when you try to learn everything during the last week before the final exam.

4. *Study and really* learn the math; don't practice mimicking it.

5. *When it's time* to register for the next session, register immediately so you'll be able to get into the math class you need. Why do all this? Because, again, math is sequential!

Math as a Sequential Course

Now that you understand the "building block" nature of math, think about your math history.

- What are your previous math grades?
- How well did you do on the math placement test at your college?
- How long has it been since you took a math course?
- When you look at your math history, are there times when you did not take math?

These questions are important because if you allow too much time to pass between different math courses, you may forget important concepts that you'll need in a future class. In other words, your foundation might require a few repairs. This means that it's incredibly important to take a math placement test before enrolling for any college-level math course.

Math placement test scores are determined by how well you've learned previous math and whether the sequence in which you took your previous courses has helped you build a strong foundation. If you barely score high enough to be placed into a math course, then you'll have gaps in your knowledge base. Learning problems then occur when new math material is based on one of these gaps.

In addition to considering how well you place into a course, the age of the placement test score must also be considered. Placement test scores are designed to measure your current math knowledge and are best used immediately. If your college does not require a placement test, or if you are in a co-requisite course, then ask you instructor how your math skills can be assessed based on the reasons stated above."

Example: While a student can maintain success by taking U.S. History I and then waiting a year to take U.S. History II, taking Beginning Algebra and then taking Intermediate Algebra a year later decreases his or her course success rate by 20%, according to Miami Dade College research.

Other research indicates that even skipping one session greatly decreases math course success rates. The same problem has also been documented at Rutgers University where students were allowed to take their developmental courses whenever they wanted. Many of these students took developmental courses during their freshman year, then waited to finish their math courses as seniors. This caused major problems as the students forgot everything they learned and still needed over a year of math courses to graduate. After conducting this research, the university implemented a policy requiring students to continuously enroll in their math courses to improve their course success rate.

College math courses should be taken in order, from the fall session to the spring session. If possible, avoid taking math from the spring to fall sessions. It is easy to forget important concepts over summer break. Summer math courses are also a good idea, unless the sessions are very short. Extended summer sessions, which typically last between 10 and 12 weeks, are preferable to waiting three months to take another course. If you cannot take summer math courses, make sure to review the last chapter in your last course to refresh your memory during your vacation. If you do not have your text, consider visiting math websites or downloading math apps. This will better prepare you to make a good grade in your next math course.

Math as a Thinking Subject

In a math class, you have to think from the minute the instructor begins talking. Note taking is challenging because you have to think about the math as your instructor explains a problem, all while writing the information down in your notes. In most cases, you're not just copying down facts. This could cause problems in note taking because you're concentrating on understanding the explanation while also trying to write down each problem step.

Also, students must think when reading the math textbook, which is why it takes longer than reading other texts. Remember when I said math is sequential?

Math is a series of steps and combinations of rules and properties. You have to think between each step, remembering the rules and properties you've learned throughout your entire collegiate career. When reading a math textbook, take time to think how each new concept connects with the previous one. This slows the reading process down significantly.

Since math is a thinking subject, what should you do?

1. *Reserve much more* time to read a chapter or complete your homework.
2. *During the evenings* or days when you don't have time to complete the entire homework assignment, at least review your notes and do a couple of problems to keep the information in your brain.
3. *You need to learn* how to think like a math instructor. This means you need to think in a step-by-step way to solve problems, writing down each step of the problem without skipping steps until the problem is solved.

Math as a Speed Subject

In most cases, math is taught faster than your other subjects. Math instructors have a certain amount of material to cover each session. They have to finish certain chapters because the next math course is based on the information taught in their courses. In many cases, math departments give a common final exam to gauge your readiness for your next course.

Another way math is a speed subject is that most math tests are timed. This causes many students to fear that they will not finish. THIS OFTEN CREATES PANIC! What makes me curious is, if students feel like they don't have enough time to complete the math test, why are most of them gone before the test time is over? Sure, students who have learned the math thoroughly may complete the test early. That makes sense. Some students leave, however, because they don't know the material, they want to leave the anxious environment, or they carelessly work through the test.

So, since speed is an issue in learning math, what should you do?

First, to use an analogy, start a daily workout program to stay in shape. Review, review, review as you learn and digest new material.

Second, practice doing problems within a time constraint. This prepares your for upcoming tests.

The Differences Between High School and College Math

Math, as a college-level course, is almost two to three times as difficult as high school-level math courses. There are many reasons for the increased difficulty: course class-time, the amount of material covered, the length of a course, and the grading system, among others. College math instruction for the fall and spring sessions is usually three hours per week; high school math instruction is usually provided in five hours per week. What is learned in one year of high school math is learned in one session of college math. Simply put, in college, students receive less instructional time per week and instructors cover twice the material per course. As a result, most of the learning occurs outside of the college classroom.

Example: Algebra II and Intermediate Algebra are similar courses. High school students take Algebra II for about nine months, five hours a week, totaling about 200 hours. College students take Intermediate Algebra for about 16 weeks for three hours a week which is 48 hours.

During orientation sessions, I often ask students how much time they used to spend studying for math in high school. Most answer that they'd studied between one and five hours. Others tell me that they paid attention in class, barely studied, and still managed to pass. This method DOES NOT WORK in college. In order to succeed in a college-level math course, you must study at least 10 hours per week. This sounds like a lot, but when broken down into one or two hour study sessions, the time is not so intimidating.

Course-Grading System

While in high school, if you make a borderline D/F in a math course, your teacher might give you a "D," and you may continue to the next course. However, in some college math courses, a "D" is not considered a passing grade, or, if a "D" is made, the course will not count toward graduation. College instructors are more likely to give the grade of "N" (no grade), "W" (withdrawal), or "F" for barely knowing the material. Instructors know students are unable to pass the next course if they have learned only a part of the curriculum. Also, in most high schools, you may graduate by passing one to three math courses. Some college programs require four math courses, and students must make at least a "C" in all of them to graduate.

What should you not expect in a college math course? Since math is not subjective, do not expect to talk a math instructor into extra credit work. Also, in college, there are no "daily work" grades. Don't expect to do well without doing the homework even though it is not collected. Finally, test scores may be the only grades that count toward your final grade. Therefore, do not assume you'll be able to "make up" for a bad test score.

Putting Math Into Perspective

One way to change the way you learn math is to compare it to one of your favorite hobbies or extracurricular activities. This will inspire you to apply the same effort level to it as you would your favorite hobby. The following activities all relate to math in fundamental ways.

Math as a Puzzle

Have you ever tried to put a puzzle together with one or more of the pieces missing? It becomes very frustrating, especially if you think all the parts are there and, after hours and hours of work, you realize you won't be able to finish. Puzzles are fickle that way. Each piece is crucial. If even a single piece is missing, you're left with an incomplete picture. This is also true when you're halfway through solving a math problem and find out you do not know or have forgotten the rules for the next step. In order to solve math problems, you need to understand all the rules. In other subjects, you may forget some of the rules and still pass a test. In math, however, not knowing or forgetting one major concept often causes you to miss problems.

Math as a Foreign Language

Another way to properly study math is to treat it as a foreign language. Like a foreign language, math has unfamiliar vocabulary words, which must be put in sentences called "expressions" or "equations." Understanding and solving a math equation is similar to speaking and understanding a sentence in a foreign language. When read or spoken aloud, mathematical symbols are translated into words and sentences. Math sentences use symbols (spoken words), such as:

"=" (for which you say, "equals"),
"-" (for which you say, "less"), and
"a" (for which you say, "unknown").

If you do not understand these symbols, you are in serious trouble. This is best illustrated by the experiences of a student named Charlie, whom I once worked with. While preparing for a math test, Charlie memorized how to work every type of problem his teacher had covered in the previous weeks. Despite his efforts, he still failed. When I went over the test with him, I asked him how to factor a polynomial. He asked me, "What's a polynomial?" I then asked him what a monomial was, and he did not know. I talked to his tutor and the rest of the tutoring session was spent learning the language of mathematics by developing vocabulary notecards so he could understand what we were talking about. He had the ability to do math but could not understand the language. Learning how to speak math as a language is key to success. With this in mind, to stay fluent in a foreign language, you need to use it every day. Math is no different. If you want to retain your ability to speak and read mathematics, you must practice every single day.

So, now that you know math is like a foreign language, what should you do?

1. *Start a vocabulary* list in the back of your notebook. Include the definitions and examples the instructor uses in class. Writing this vocabulary list helps you study too!

2. *Preview the chapter* before class in order to identify vocabulary words that you will hear in class. You don't have to understand all of them while previewing the chapter, but familiarize yourself with the words. This will help you improve taking notes in class.

3. *Practice saying* the vocabulary words out loud. Get comfortable with the words, their meanings, and how they connect with one another.

Math as a Sport

Learning math is similar to learning to play a sport such as basketball, track or football. In order to find success, you must actively practice. You can listen and watch your coach all day, but unless you practice those skills yourself, you will not learn and probably won't even get into the game or meet.

For example, in basketball, the way to improve your free-throw percentage is to watch and understand the correct shooting form and then to actively practice the shots. If you simply listen to your coaches describe

the correct form and watch them demonstrate it, but you do not practice the correct form yourself, you will never improve.

Math as a Musical Instrument

Learning math is like playing a musical instrument. To master a musical instrument, you need to understand music theory and learn the various hand-eye movements required to strike the right sound and tone.

This involves lots of practice. You can see someone play the piano, cello or electric guitar, watch their hands and hear the sounds, but unless you practice, you will not learn how to play. Imagine how many concerts you've attended or seen on television, or how many people you've watched play the piano. Could you now go play the piano, cello or electric guitar? No. You need to practice these instruments before playing them well just like you have to practice math before you learn it.

Many of your other college courses can be learned by methods other than practicing. In social studies, for example, you can learn information by listening to your instructor, taking good notes and participating in class discussions. Many first-year college students mistakenly believe they can approach math the same way. Ask an experienced math student, and you'll hear a different story. Face it, unless you are a math genius, you must practice. So, how do you practice math?

- *First,* make sure you understand the math concepts and the basics.

- *Second,* practice the homework problems over and over until the answers come to you naturally.

- *Third,* learn the vocabulary associated with problems.

- *Fourth,* try to "teach" the math to someone else.

Activity 1.3 Studying Math is like...

One of the best ways to study for math is to treat it the same way you would one of your favorite hobbies or performance-based activities. Not to say that you need to enjoy math the same way you enjoy playing basketball or singing or playing an instrument, but you certainly need to give it the same type of attention. Answer the questions below to find out how you can use your experiences participating in an activity you love to shape or reshape your approach to math.

1. Which one of the comparisons in this section is the most relatable to you? Do you play a musical instrument? Have you ever taken a foreign language class? Have you ever played a sport? Choose one of the comparisons and explain how you can use it to improve your study habits.

2. If none of the comparisons given in this section apply to you, think of one of your hobbies or activities and explain below how you can use your practice routine for this activity as an example for how to properly study math.

3. Explain, in your own words, why it is important to consistently study for math. What, for instance, makes studying for math unique?

How to Take Control of Your College Math Experience

The best ways to take control over math are to develop an internal locus of control, to avoid learned helplessness, and to eliminate (or at least decrease) procrastination. This is first accomplished by setting short-term goals. Accomplishing these goals allows you to see the relationship between positive learning behavior and mathematics success. You can then develop long-term goals such as making an "A" or "B" in your math class or graduating college.

Defining Locus of Control

Locus of control has to do with the locus, or location, in which a student places the control over his or her life; or, in other words, who or what a student feels controls his or her behavior and grades. Students who feel that conditions beyond their control prevent them from getting good grades have an *external* locus of control. These students blame instructors, home conditions and money problems for their poor grades. In essence, external students feel their lives are controlled by outside forces, such as fate or the power of other people. They often believe that these problems are beyond their control.

Other students feel that they have the power to control their situation, and this power comes from within. These *internal* students take responsibility for their success, while most external students reject responsibility. Internal students believe that they can overcome most situations, since results depend on their behavior or personal characteristics. Internal students accept responsibility for their behavior and realize that studying today will help them pass the math test scheduled for next week. Internal students can delay immediate rewards. Instead of going to a party, they study for tomorrow's test. Internal students also know when to postpone putting in extra hours at their workplace in order to study for a math test.

Generally, locus of control means that students who are internal will work harder to meet their educational goals than will external students. The internal student can relate today's behavior (e.g., studying, textbook reading) to obtaining a college degree and gainful employment.

On the other hand, external students cannot connect the behavior of studying today with getting passing grades and obtaining future career opportunities. Thus, internal students are more oriented toward making high math grades than are externals.

Self-Esteem

Many students experience problems in both their academic and personal lives because they lack self-esteem. Self-esteem is the part of our personality which allows us to feel good about ourselves and enjoy our accomplishments. Having self-esteem means that you respect others and have a sense of peace within yourself. Students who have self-esteem also have a "can do" attitude about accomplishing their goals.

Students with poor self-esteem may not put forth as much effort to accomplish their goals. These students can improve their self-esteem by taking responsibility for their feelings, thoughts, abilities, and behaviors. Students with poor self-esteem need to change their negative emotional reactions into positive emotional reactions.

Improving self-esteem can be accomplished by changing the negative emotional statements you sometimes tell yourself and by changing bad behaviors that result in a lack of self respect. By developing positive short-term goals, you change the behaviors that are associated with poor self-esteem. Negative emotional statements are often referred to as "negative self-talk."

It is possible to change these negative statements to positive ones. List your negative self-talk statements starting with "I" and change them to positive "I" statements. For example, when starting a new math class, instead of telling yourself, "I hope I don't fail," tell yourself, "When I do well at something, I am going to congratulate myself." To practice this process, see activity 1.4.

Productive Persistence

Productive persistence is another term associated with math success. The Carnegie Foundation defines it as the tenacity and good strategies students need to become more successful. According to the Carnegie Foundation's research, the combination of tenacity and good study strategies is a formula for math success.

Tenacious students work hard, study the appropriate amount of hours, make learning a priority, and postpone immediate self-gratification for long-term success in math. These student remain in math classes and do not withdraw at the first sign of difficulty. They also develop short-term and long-term goals. This allows them to see the progress they make even when they hit a stumbling block. You can improve your tenacity by applying the motivational and goal setting suggestions in this chapter.

The good strategies part of this successful formula involves learning and using math study skills. Those students who use general study skills often study 15 to 20 hours a week on math without any success. I call these students "wheel spinners." By not learning math-specific study skills, these students are in effect riding a stationary bike. They are putting in a whole lot of work, but they aren't going anywhere. The math study skills you will learn in this text have been proven to improve math success.

Self-Learning

Math courses require students to learn a great deal of information outside of class. Luckily, modern math students have more tools at their disposal than ever before. Over the course of this text, we will introduce you to numerous supplementary tools that will help you learn complex mathematical concepts.

Some of these resources are physical locations on your campus, others are Web-based research tools. If you want continued success, it's important to keep up with and use these tools.

Mindfulness and Success

From the very first week of college orientation until the hectic week of graduation, college life is full of opportunities and responsibilities. It does not matter if you live on campus or commute. It does not matter if you're single, married, with or without parental responsibilities. Balancing opportunities and responsibilities is key to academic success. That's why just about every college orientation textbook has a chapter on values, goals, and time management. One ability successful students use continuously is the ability to manage these opportunities and responsibilities so that they do not become distractions. There's another powerful source for distractions—our minds.

The mind can be our worst enemy or our closest ally. Thoughts, emotions, and sensations about previous experiences or future ones can serve as our looking glass into the present. As the worst enemy, a present situation triggers old thoughts and emotions that cause us to handle the present in ways that we further harm ourselves. As our closest ally, when emotions and thoughts about what is happening around us disrupt our ability to focus, the mind can learn to stop these internal distractions and improve concentration in the present.

One of the most successful strategies is practicing the mental state called mindfulness. Mindfulness is the ability to interact with the present moment with full attention, without allowing thoughts, internal dialogue, and accompanying emotions to interfere with how we interact in the present.

Sounds great, even somewhat simplistic, but it takes time and the desire to work with anxiety instead of avoiding it. It means a student with high math anxiety must live with it. So, instead of delving into the "how to's," we need to explore the benefits of mindfulness.

1. Anxiety minimizes the ability to learn. Anxious intrusive thoughts while completing math problems decrease speed and accuracy (Brunye, Mahone, et. 2013) Students with too much anxiety cannot remain focused while studying, so they waste precious time. Mindfulness consists of strategies to remove the source of anxiety and thus the anxious emotion from the present moment.

2. For many students, math anxiety is embarrassing, thus they try to hide it. A key concept in mindfulness is that anxiety is the same as any other emotion. Anxiety, like all other emotions, does not define who you are unless you let it. When learning to develop a state of mindfulness, people learn to accept anxiety as an emotion, while also learning to love themselves (even with anxiety).

3. Mindfulness is not limited to math anxiety. A mental state of mindfulness enhances how we interact in any present situation, so students with math anxiety who make the effort to learn Mindfulness will improve other areas of their lives.

You can do the following steps to achieve this dimension of mindfulness immediately.

Step 1: Practice the Right Mindset.

- Non-judgement: Emotions are not good or bad. We can't judge ourselves based on the emotions we feel, even though others may.

- We are not our emotions: Emotions come and go. We are like the sky and emotions are the clouds. Sometimes there are dark gray storm clouds and other times white fluffy ones. None of them stay in the sky forever. When we feel nervous or anxious, we tell ourselves that it's not going to last.

- Avoidance does not work in this situation. We can't keep ourselves from feeling emotions. We must learn how to interact with them. It's almost like personifying the emotion and setting it to the side, then deciding what we are going to do with it.

- Self-respect and self-love: We cannot allow our minds to beat us up. There are enough tangible stressors to manage. We do not want to battle our emotions too. We must learn to accept our emotions, in this case anxiety, and manage them in ways that they do not interfere with studying.

Step 2: Learn how to react to anxiety when it first creeps into the mind:

- When you notice it, say, "I'm beginning to feel some anxiety." Whether you know why or do not, say, "I need to deal with this issue and the anxiety, but for now I must set it aside."

- The following ideas seem corny, but they can work. Take a piece of paper, wad it up, and as you throw it in the waste basket, say, "Not now. Not going to happen. I have time to deal with it later." Each time anxiety or pre-occupation of any kind is interfering, throw another piece of paper in the waste basket. You can do this before a math class, studying alone or in a lab. When you take a math test, throw the paper wad into the basket before the test.

- Breathe deeply several times and as you inhale think of a positive outcome for completing the study task. Keep this thought inside you as you hold your breath for a few seconds. Then exhale and relax your body.

Step 3: Use interactive study strategies while studying

- Create test review notecards while learning new math concepts, rules, and formulas. Each card should include definition, how it is used, steps, and example(s). Keep these cards in your room. Take pictures of each card with your phone, so when you have a few extra minutes, you can review them.

- Try studying in a math center, study center, library or other places where you can concentrate but not be alone. The mind is less likely to begin on a destructive path when you are not alone.

- Find someone to study with a few times a week. If you live off campus, use available technology to connect and study with others in your class.

Step 4: Get some sun and exercise.

- It only takes fifteen to twenty minutes of sun each day to lift the spirits. If possible, let the sun hit your arms or legs so that the body can absorb vitamin D. This could happen just by walking to class, walking the dog, or playing with your kids outside.

Step 5: Do not participate in avoidance

- Emotions come and go, but that does not mean we should ignore them. Anxiety comes in different forms and levels of intensity. If anxiety is controlling you right now, do not wait to read Chapter Five on math and test anxiety. Read it now. Also, seek out professional assistance, so an expert can coach you throughout the semester on how to minimize the anxiety and manage it.

Activity 1.4 Taking Control of Your Math Experience

Math students have various perceived levels of math control. Even the best students need to develop strategies to improve motivation and control over math. This is first accomplished by setting up short-term goals. To get started, follow the directions below:

1. List and describe how you would use two locus of control concepts and one self-efficacy concept for motivation and controlling your math experience.

     a.

     b.

2. List and describe how you would use two productive persistence strategies to control your math experience.

     a.

     b.

3. List and describe how you would improve your self-esteem by changing negative math self-talk statements into positive statement to improve motivation. First, list the negative statement, then list the positive self statement to take its place.

     Negative statement:

     Positive statement:

     Negative statement:

     Positive statement:

4. Describe what mindfulness means to you. Then list five mindful thoughts/behaviors that can help control your anxiety and help you control math. Ex: " I will not let my mind beat me up about math:

Mindfulness to me is:

Thoughts/behaviors:
a.

b.

c.

d.

e.

How to Improve Your Math Self-Efficacy

Self-efficacy is another term colleges and universities often use. This term is related to locus of control but is more specific to certain tasks. Locus of control is an overall belief that you can be successful. Generally speaking, self-efficacy is more specific to the belief that you have the abilities or skills to complete certain tasks (Bandura, 1982). To determine self-efficacy, ask yourself this question by filling in the blank: "Do I have the skills and ability to succeed at _____." The blank could include tasks such as employment, an English course, a history course, a math course, or graduating from college.

Just like in locus of control, educational research has found that self-efficacy is an important success predictor of student motivation and self-management behavior (Schunk, 1991). A more recent article showed that study skills and study skills courses can improve academic self-efficacy (Wernersbock, 2014). This is important, as students with high efficacy are more likely than students with low efficacy to complete difficult tasks, to put in more effort, to show persistence, to have used different learning strategies, and to have less fear about completing a task. In short, these students believe they can complete tasks such as taking notes, reading the textbook, completing their homework, and managing their time. They persist at these skills until proficient.

Math self-efficacy is a specific type of self-efficacy that involves your belief that you can perform certain math tasks and become successful in mathematics. Recent research suggests that this belief is extremely important. In 2017, a group of educators— Zientek, Fong and Phelps—concluded that about 38% of successful math skills and learning comes from math self-efficacy. This mostly has to do with the affective characteristics we discussed earlier. So how can we use the results of this research to help you improve your success in math?

You can improve your math self-efficacy in two major areas. One involves you, the student; the other involves the classroom or lab. The rest of this section will help you with this by describing how four different aspects of self-efficacy affect these two areas: mastery experiences, vicarious experiences, social persuasions, and psychological states.

Mastery Experiences

Mastery experience is based on previous math experience and successfully completing problems and tests. There are two goals, here. First, you want to be able to ask questions confidently in the classroom about solving problems and obtain a better understanding of concepts. Second, you want to walk out of the classroom fully confident that you can solve problems. If you achieve these goals, you'll move forward with a newfound trust in your own abilities that will almost certainly improve your grades.

So how should you create these experiences if you think you aren't good at math? The short answer is to go get help. If you can't solve certain problems during class or while doing homework, take them to the math lab. Ask the tutor to help you solve the problems and make sure before leaving the lab that you have solved several problems successfully.

Another way to boost your confidence is to always end a classroom, study, or homework session on a high note. When you finish writing down problem steps during class, for instance, praise yourself for successfully taking notes. Or, if you're doing online math homework, make sure you successfully finish your last problems before quitting. The key is to carry forward confident vibes into your next math experience.

If you struggle with math and see these sort of confidence boosters as unlikely, fret not! If you use the anxiety reduction and test-taking skills in this text, you will have the skills you need to improve. Look at the results of your Math Study Skills Evaluation. If you did poorly, that is great! Now you can tell yourself that your lack of study skills is the major obstacle to having positive experiences with math. It has nothing to do with your intelligence; you just need better tools. With this in mind, don't wait to go to the pages suggested in the evaluation. Start learning these skills now!

Vicarious Experiences

The term "vicarious experiences" sounds fancy, but it's actually quite simple. It refers to when you realize that you have things in common with other successful students—in other words, when you meet students from similar backgrounds who are good at math.

The importance of this cannot be overstated. When in class, it is crucial to meet students you feel comfortable with and start a study group with them. This might include students who once struggled with math but

have since figured out how to thrive in their courses. If someone in this group inspires you, great! Know that you are just as capable of finding success. If no one sticks out in your class in this way, ask your tutors or instructors about students who have turned things around in the past. I'm sure they have many stories like this. Having worked with math students for decades, I have hundreds of stories about students who had poor math backgrounds becoming successful. All it took was effort, self-confidence, and study skills!

Social Persuasion

Social persuasion involves discussions you may have that enhance or diminish your math self-efficacy. It is important to associate with students who have positive attitudes and statements about math. This doesn't mean that you and your classmates aren't allowed to complain about bad past experiences, but it is extremely important that your overall discussion about math is positive. Try to avoid talking to overly negative students. For example, if you are sitting at a table in the math lab where students are all doom and gloom about their chances of passing their courses, sit somewhere else! Find a more positive table!

As for what you can do as an individual, seek out tutors or instructors that give timely and constructive feedback. This feedback helps you increase your effort to improve. Also, use the mindfulness, mindset, and locus of control strategies discussed earlier in this chapter to create your own positive feedback. While external motivation is great, it is just as important to tell yourself that you're capable of thriving in your math courses.

Physiological States

This concept mainly deals with math, test, and homework anxiety. As a rule, anxiety is bad for self-efficacy. As anxiety increases, self-efficacy decreases. This means that it is important to ease any nervousness or trauma when heading into stressful situations. Talk to your instructor, tutor, advisor, or counselor about your anxiety and ask for strategies to help reduce it. For more read Chapter Five of this text.

Mindset Concepts

Using mindset concepts is another way to improve self-efficacy. Mindset is different from mindfulness. There are two types: fixed and growth. A fixed mindset means that you believe your ability to learn certain subjects is set in stone and can't be improved. A growth mindset means that you believe yourself capable of change and improvement (Dweck, 2016).

Mindsets are important because a growth mindset leads to different learning behaviors that change the biochemical pathways in the brain that affect learning and memory. This occurs because students with growth mindset understand how hard work and persistence lead to success. This knowledge literally changes the way they think and behave. They are much more likely to work through difficulties, study as long as it takes to master material, and continue to improve even after they've scored a victory or two on tests. Indeed, countless students have used a growth mind set to help improve their mathematical learning (Boaler, 2016).

To adopt this mindset, you must develop study skills that will boost your confidence and self-efficacy. This text covers many of these strategies, and you should not be afraid to try them out. Don't wait for your instructor to assign the anxiety chapter. Go ahead and read it, then start practicing what you learn.

Before reading this text, you may not have had these skills and may have suffered from low math self-efficacy. Now, you can use these learning and test-taking skills to improve your math self-efficacy, which will lead to more motivation to become successful in your current and future courses. They really do help!

Activity 1.5 Improving Math Self-Efficacy

Improving math self-efficacy should be a goal of every student. After reading this section, you may have some idea how to do this. To get started, follow the directions below on a blank sheet of paper.

1. Describe what math self-efficacy means to you.

2. Write down one Master Experiences strategy and how you will apply it to yourself.
    a. Strategy:
    b. Application: I will …

3. Write down one Vicarious Experience strategy and how you will apply it to yourself.
    a. Strategy:
    b. Application: I will ….

4. Write down one Social Persuasion strategy and how you will apply it to yourself.
    a. Strategy:
    b. Application: I will…

5. Write down one Physiological States strategy and how you will apply it to yourself.
    a. Strategy:
    b. Application: I will…

6. Develop a plan: Decide which applications you will try first, second, third and fourth. Which applications worked best for your and why?

How to Communicate with Your Professor

Communicating with your math instructor can help you gain control over math. However, many students find this difficult in and out of class. Some fear talking to their instructors, while others simply don't see the need to communicate with them at all.

Most of this fear is based on past experiences. Students often indicate that going to their math instructor is like going to the principal's office. Even if you had a poor experience attempting to communicate with an instructor in the past, that does not mean you'll have the same experience with your current instructor. In fact, math instructors want you to learn the material and want to see you succeed. Why else would they have chosen teaching as a profession? One of the biggest complaints among math instructors is that students do not ask questions in class and do not take advantage of office hours to receive additional help. If you are one of these students, then you need to take control and realize that communicating with your math instructor is essential to your success.

You should begin communicating with your instructor in class immediately. Be sure to ask any questions you may have about the syllabus early in the course. If you have any questions about math concepts as they are being presented, ask them. Remember, if you have a question about something, chances are other students in the class have the same

question but are afraid to ask it.

Also, be sure to communicate with your professor outside of class early in the semester. At the very least, you should make an effort to reach out to your professor before the first major exam. Use this time to ensure that you understand what material will be covered on the first exam and to work with the instructor to clarify any concepts you do not understand. Your first exam sets the tone for the rest of the class, so it's important to take it very seriously.

You can reach out to your math professor outside of class in several ways:

1. Call the math department office and make an appointment.

2. Visit the instructor during his/her office hours. Usually the office hours and syllabus are posted on the door.

3. Call the instructor at his/her office and speak on the phone.

4. Email the instructor

5. If your course has an online component or is fully online, use any available chat rooms, discussion boards, or other communication tools.

Now that you have decided to speak with your instructor, what do you want to discuss? Don't feel that you have to wait until you are having major problems to communicate with your instructor.

In fact, it is much better to start communication if you're having only minor issues with the material or simply need more information about the course. Here are some suggested topics for discussion:

1. The course syllabus (grading policy, attendance policy, etc.).

2. Your math background. Don't be afraid to tell him/her that you've had math problems in the past.

3. How to solve some math problems you are struggling with. Bring a short list of specific problems.

4. Additional resources that might be available such as tutoring, videos, etc.

5. Any class meetings you know that you might miss and/or how to inform the instructor in the case of absence.

6. Questions you may have about the online homework system, phone apps, or any other course materials as applicable.

Do not ask questions or make statements like these:

1. How many classes can I miss before being withdrawn?

2. Will you be giving us any extra credit in this course?

3. Are you an easy instructor?

4. When will I ever use this stuff?

5. How many times have you taught this class before?

6. Why do I have to do my homework online?

7. You explain things differently than my last instructor.

8. I looked you up on Rate My Professor.

9. This is my second time taking this class. I really need to pass this time.

10. I'm taking this class online because I thought it would be easier.

These types of questions and statements may give the instructor a bad impression of you and put him/her on the defensive. If you ensure that your questions are positive and represent you as a dedicated and involved student who is serious about succeeding in the course, then communicating with your instructor can have many benefits.

Here are just a few of them:

1. Instructors know who you are among their many other students.

2. In class, you feel more open to asking questions.

3. The instructor often answers your questions more quickly and more thoroughly than those from other students, and it becomes easier to meet with the instructor if more difficult questions or serious issues arise.

4. Your instructor is able to identify your problem areas faster and target his/her explanations to your needs.

5. The instructor is often able to teach to your preferred learning preference.

6. If you have a borderline grade, the instructor may have a reason to give you the higher of the two grades based on your level of dedication.

7. The instructor may recognize your genuine desire to succeed and take longer answering your questions, particularly in an online class or in e-mail responses.

8. Your instructor may become someone you can visit in the future for additional help in other courses or to write you letters of recommendation.

The bottom line is that positive, ongoing communication with your instructor improves math learning and even math grades. DO NOT BE AFRAID! Use your internal locus of control and math self-efficacy to reach out to your instructor and communicate early and often. Your instructor wants you to succeed just as much as you do!

Chapter One: Checklist for Knowledge and Behaviors

Put a check after understanding the knowledge statements and fill in the behavioral activities.

Chapter Knowledge

1. I understand that persistence is one of the key factors to math success. _____
2. I understand that math requires sequential learning, which means that one concept builds on the next. I must build a firm foundation with each chapter to help me succeed. _____
3. I understand that one of the major differences between high school and college math is that most learning occurs outside the classroom. This means that I need to study more. _____
4. I think that learning math is like learning a foreign language, playing sports, or practicing a musical instrument. _____
5. I understand that math is an active subject, and I must practice it by doing my homework. ___
6. I understand that the skills required for learning math differ from the skills required for learning other subjects. _____
7. I understand that passing most courses requires reading, understanding, and recalling information; however, math students must generalize concepts by thinking like their instructor. _____
8. I know that I can dislike math and pass it at the same time. _____
9. I will go to math class every class day. _____
10. I understand how math self-efficacy can improve my math success. ____
11. I visited my instructor the first or second week of class. _____
12. I developed motivational strategies for myself. _____

Behavioral Activities

1. I completed and reviewed the Math Study Skills Evaluation—7th Edition with a total score of _____.
2. I know that my last math grade was a _____ and have not taken math in _____ months. I believe I have a good math foundation or one that needs some repairs (circle one). Circling "needs some repair" means that I will immediately go to the math lab.
3. I studied _____ hours a week for math in high school and will study _____ hours a week for math in college.
4. I know math is not just numbers, so I started a math vocabulary list in the back of my note book on / / .
5. I found out from the career center that my major will need _____ math course(s), and I will make $_____.

Name: _____   Date: _____

Assignment for Chapter 1

Answer the following questions on a separate piece of paper.

1. Why is math considered to have a sequential learning pattern?

2. Give two examples of how math is a speed subject.

3. Give three examples of how college math is different from high school math.

4. Define "Productive Persistence" and how you obtain this characteristic.

5. Define "self-esteem," then list and define five ways you can improve your self-esteem.

6. Define "mindfulness" and list three mindfulness strategies you can use to improve math success.

7. How can positive and negative attitudes toward math affect learning?

8. Describe three personal obstacles that may prevent you from learning more math.

9. List one strategy per obstacle (listed above) that you will use to overcome it.

10. Explain two reasons why some students don't want to communicate with their instructor, as well as two ways you will communicate with your instructor before your first test.

How to Improve Listening and Note-Taking Skills

In Chapter 2
You will learn these concepts:

- ✓ How to listen effectively and identify important concepts

- ✓ How to design a classroom note-taking system

- ✓ How to build online and computer-based note-taking systems

- ✓ How to take notes with technology

- ✓ How creating a math glossary improves learning

How to Become an Effective Listener

Listening and note-taking skills in a math class are very important, since most students do not read the math text or have difficulty understanding it. In most of your other classes, if you do not understand the lecture, you can read the book and get almost all the information. In the math class, however, the instructor can usually explain the textbook better than students can read and understand it. Students who do not have good listening skills or note-taking skills are at a disadvantage in learning math. Most math understanding takes place in the classroom. Students must learn how to take advantage of learning in the classroom by becoming effective listeners, technology users, and note-takers.

You can become an effective listener using a set of skills, which you can learn and practice. To do this, you must prepare both physically and mentally.

It's also important to point out, students are now receiving their lectures online. For example, you may be in a computer-based classroom or taking an online course. Both of these systems feature math lectures online, so you cannot ask instructors questions. This type of delivery system requires an entirely different type of note-taking in order to learn material.

Warming Up for Math Class

The first step of mental preparation for note-taking involves "warming up" before class. Just as an athlete must "warm up" before a game, you must "warm up" before taking notes. "Warm up" by reviewing the previous day's notes, reviewing the reading material, reviewing the homework, preparing questions, or reworking one or two problems done in the previous class.

This mental "warm up" before the lecture refreshes your memory, making it easier to learn new material. Students who "warm up" are "ready to go" as soon as the instructor starts lecturing, and they keep up with what is discussed in class.

How to Become an Active Listener and Learner

In many ways, math class is like a race. Every session follows the same pattern:

1. *On your mark* — sit in your desk.
2. *Get set* — get focused and be ready to take notes when the instructor begins.
3. *Go* — keep a steady pace with note-taking.
4. *Last lap* — stay focused, even if you're tired.

5. *Finish line*—class is over. You have good notes. Time to practice for your next race.

In order to complete this process, you must become an active listener. Active listening means integrating the thinking and learning process with listening and recording information.

First, it involves learning the instructor's lecture style, how he or she indicates when information is important. What information does he or she tend to leave out? Is it best to keep the book open during lecture? How parallel is the lecture with the book? The pace of the instructor's lecture is important. If it's too slow, you must think of ways to remain focused like finding sample problems in the book. If it's too fast, you must find a way to make short cuts in recording information while still getting the details.

Second, you must be a participant in the class. Ask questions. Listen to other students' questions. Be willing to ask questions for clarification when confused because if you're confused, so is someone else. Questions are another way to force an instructor to repeat information or provide more details. Sometimes it's easy to fall into the frame of mind where you just go to class and get the notes down, planning to learn it later. That is passive listening. No more sitting in the back, slouched in the desk, waiting to write whatever the instructor puts on the board.

What do you think about while in math class? First, listen for the instructor to discuss what you learned when you previewed the chapter. If you have a book, it helps to have it open to the chapter the instructor is talking about. You can compare the information from the lecture with the book or later on with a video or web/app resources.

Second, if the instructor is speeding on, ask a question to help you understand what is being discussed. This also gives a mental break for everyone. Just don't ask too many questions that are irrelevant. Classmates do not appreciate those questions.

Third, as the instructor explains how to do something, listen for the explanation of why particular steps are completed. If you don't hear the "why," be brave and ask. Usually the answer will include the rules, properties or laws that explain why certain steps are taken. This will help you and many of your classmates understand what's going on. Make sure you record this information in your notes.

There will be times when the instructor has to present so much information at a fast pace, all you can do is make sure you get it down. One trick is to sit next to someone who is trying to listen as intently as you. When one of you spaces out, the other one will still be focused and getting the notes down. At the end of class, compare notes and fill in each other's gaps. If you can, sit close enough to look at each other's notes to fill in gaps. This is particularly helpful in a class that meets for a long time. The catch is that in these situations, you must review the notes as soon as possible because you didn't have as much time to think about the information in class.

So how do you go about reviewing your notes as soon as possible? I have asked this question to many students and have never accepted the answer that they did not have enough time. If you try hard enough, you can always find enough time to review your notes. Try to find time between your classes or during lunch. Even better, get to your next class early and use the quiet time before class to go over everything you just wrote. Even three to five minutes of review improves learning. This is time incredibly well spent. Not only are you embedding fresh information into your memory, you're actively studying for future exams.

Remember, class time should be considered a valuable study period where you listen, take notes, and learn at the same time. One way to learn more in class is to memorize important facts when the instructor is talking about material you already know. Another technique is to repeat back to yourself important concepts right after the instructor says them in class. Using class time to learn math is an efficient learning system.

Activity 2.1   Assessing Your Listening Strengths

Now that you have become an effective listener, it is time to assess what strategies you have been using and which strategies you can use to improve these skills. In the section below, answer the questions and then compare your answers to a classmate's.

1.   What 'warm up strategies' have you been using in your math class?

2.   With this new information, what new strategies can you use to "warm up" for your math class?

3.   What active learning strategies have you been using in your math class?

4.   What new active learning strategies can you use in your math class?

5.   The progression of a math class is very similar to a race. After each race stage below, put a personal statement starting with "I will" on how you will complete that stage.

   a. On your mark —

   b. Get set —

   c. Go —

   d. Last lap —

   e. Finish line —

How to Become an Effective Classroom Note-Taker

Becoming a good note-taker requires two basic strategies. One strategy is to be specific in detail. In other words, copy the problems down, step by step. The second strategy is to listen for the general principles, general concepts, and general ideas, and record them in your notes.

Copying from the Board

While taking math notes, you need to copy each and every step of each problem on the board, even though you may already know them. While in the classroom, you might understand each step, but a week later you might not remember unless all the steps were written down. In addition, as you write down each step, you're memorizing it. The major reason for recording every step of a problem is to understand how to do the problems while the instructor is explaining them instead of trying to remember unwritten steps when you're studying on your own. It may seem time consuming; however, it pays off during homework and test time.

There will be times when you will get lost while listening to the lecture. Nevertheless, you should keep taking notes even though you do not understand the problem. This will provide you with a reference point for further study or to ask your tutor.

Put a question mark (?) by those steps you do not understand. As you take notes on confusing problem steps, skip lines; then go back and fill in information that clarifies your misunderstanding of the steps in question at some later point. Ask your tutor or instructor for help with the uncompleted problem steps and write down the reasons for each step in the space provided.

Also, ask your professor for permission to use your smartphone to take a picture of the board. Because many phones allow panoramic photographs, it's possible to create a single image of the entire board. This method does not, however, take the place of taking proper notes. Only view the images you create as a backup or use them to ensure you copied everything down correctly.

Remember, the goal is to get all the details without writing an essay. A procedure to save time while taking notes from the board is to stop writing complete sentences. Write your main thoughts in phrases. Phrases are easier to jot down and easier to memorize. Another strategy to streamline taking notes off the board is to develop an abbreviation system.

An abbreviation system is your way to reduce long words to shorter versions, which you still can understand. By writing less, you can listen more and have a better understanding of the material. For good examples of proper abbreviations , see the chart printed below.

The Goals of Note-Taking

The goal of note-taking is to take the least amount of notes and get the greatest amount of information on your paper. This could be the opposite of what most instructors have told you. Some instructors tell you to take down everything. This is not necessarily a good note-taking system, since it's very difficult to take precise, specific notes while at the same time understanding the instructor. On the other hand, some instructors ask you to stop taking notes during a lecture and just listen. These instructors know that when explaining a major point you need to listen and not write. If you are doing both, you may not understand the important concept. Let these instructors explain the major point and then record your notes. If you didn't have enough time to take the notes, see the instructor during his/her office hours or get the notes from a friend. Getting notes from another student instead of doing your own notes is not a good idea. Notes from other students are thoughts that pertain to their math knowledge to remind them how to do problems that they don't know how to solve. You might not have the same knowledge as they do, so the notes may not help you.

Abbreviations

E.G.	(for example)
CF.	(compare, remember in context)
N.B.	(note well, this is important)
∴	(therefore)
∵	(because)
⊃	(implies, it follows from this)
>	(greater than)
<	(less than)
=	(equals, is the same)
≠	(does not equal, is not the same)
( )	(parentheses in the margin, around a sentence or group of sentences indicates an important idea)
?	(used to indicate you do not understand the material)
O	(a circle around a word may indicate that you are not familiar with it; look it up)
TQ	(marks important materials likely to be used in an exam)

1, 2, 3, 4	(to indicate a series of facts)
D	(shows disagreement with statement or passage)
REF	(reference)
et al	(and others)
bk	(book)
p	(page)
etc.	(and so forth)
V	(see)
VS	(see above)
SC	(namely)
SQ	(the following)
Comm.	(Commutative)
Dis.	(Distributive)
A.P.A.	(Associative Property of Addition)
A.I.	(Additive Inverse)
I.P.M.	(Identity Property of Multiplication)

It is best to take your own notes and compare them to a classmate's to gain additional information.

You need to develop a note-taking system in which you write the least amount possible and get the most information down while still understanding what the instructor is saying. The first step to this system is to know when to take notes.

When to Take Classroom Notes

To become a better note-taker you must know when to take notes. Instructors give cues that indicate what material is important. Some cues include:

- Presenting usual facts or ideas
- Writing on the board
- Summarizing
- Pausing
- Repeating statements
- Enumerating, such as, "1, 2, 3" or "A, B, C"
- Working several examples of the same type of problem on the blackboard
- Saying, "This is a tricky problem. Most students will miss it."
- Saying, "This is the most difficult step in the problem."
- Saying, "These types of problems will be on the test" — such as different types of word problems.
- Explaining bold-print words
- Saying, "This will be on the test."
- The instructor makes a special point of a particular PowerPoint slide, or the instructor brings up one of many Web-based resources

You must learn the cues your instructor gives indicating important material. If you're in doubt about the importance of the class material, do not hesitate to ask the instructor about its importance. If you're not sure if

something is important in the lecture, write it down just in case.

While taking notes, you may become confused about math material. At that point, take as many notes as possible, and do not give up.

When important cues indicate that this information may be on the test, make sure to put TQ (test question) in the margin of your notes. These TQs could be the instructor indicating this information will be on the test. If an instructor does the same type of problem several times and tells you that you must know how to work these types of problems, it's a TQ. These TQs need to be reviewed and learned before each test. List these TQs on a separate page in the back of your notebook to review for the test and final exam.

When to Take Online and Computer-Based Notes

If you're taking a computer-based math course, taking notes may become confusing because there may not be formal lectures. The note-taking rules have changed for these courses; however, you still need to take notes. Remember the purpose of note-taking is to provide a resource for working homework problems and preparing for tests. I have worked with hundreds of students in these types of courses who did not take notes and failed. Many had successfully completed their homework but did not have any notes or very few notes to review for the major tests. Some cues to take computer-based notes include:

1. If the instructor conducts a mini-lecture
2. If the instructor conducts a "pull out" section of students
3. When you ask for help from the class tutor or instructor
4. When you email the instructor or tutor for help on a problem
5. When it takes you three tries to get the homework problem correct
6. When you view the video lecture and don't understand the concept

Activity 2.2 Assessing Your Note-Taking Skills

Now that you have a better understanding of how to become a good note-taker, it is time to do a self-assessment to discover your strengths and those areas in which you need to improve.

1. Show your math notes to a classmate and see if he or she can read and understand the notes. Write down what they said about your notes.

2. List the type of math abbreviations you use in your notes:

3. Make up some math abbreviations you can use for your notes, and write them below:

4. What cues do you need to listen for when you take notes?

5. Based on reading this section, list five additional cues you can use to take notes:

The Seven Steps to Taking Notes in Math Class

Since most students are not court reporters, the key to effective note-taking is to record the fewest words while retaining the greatest amount of information. As you know, it's very difficult to record notes and, at the same time, fully understand your instructor. The "Seven Steps to Math Note-taking" system was developed to decrease the amount of words you write down and to maximize your math learning.

The system consists of three major components. Steps One through Three focus on recording your notes. Steps Four through Six focus on checking yourself to see how much information is retained. This is done by recalling key words and concepts and putting a check mark by misunderstood information. Recalling information is one of the best learning techniques. Step Seven, the third component, is a math glossary.

Before we get into the specifics of these steps, however, let's first explore how to set up your notes page. Great notebooks are organized and legible; they follow and stick to a singular design.

One of the best math note-taking methods is demonstrated in the figure on the next page. The "Modified Three Column Note-Taking Method" allows you to record everything you need to know to solve math problems in an easy-to-follow guide.

To set up this system, do the following on regular notebook paper:

1. *Label the top space* between the notebook ring and the red line, "Key Words."

2. *Label the other side* of the red line, "Examples."

3. *Next, label "Explanations/ Rules"* about four inches from the red line.

4. *Draw a vertical line* between the "Examples" and "Explanations/Rules" sections.

5. *Record the same information* on the next 10 pages. After using this system for 10 pages, you may not need to label each page.

Modified Three Column Note-Taking Method

Key Words/Rules	Examples	Explanations
Solve a linear equation	$5(x + 4) + 3(x - 4) = 2(x - 2)$	Have to get x on one side of the = and numbers on the other side of the =.
Distributive Property	$5x + 20 + 3x - 12 = 2x-4$	Multiply numbers to the left of the ( ) by each variable and number in the ( ).
Commutative Property	$5x + 3x + 20 - 12 = 2x-4$	Regroup numbers and variables.
Combine like terms	$8x + 8 = 2x - 4$	Add x's together and numbers together .
Additive Inverse Property	$8x - 2x + 8 = 2x - 2x -4$ $6x + 8 = -4$	Subtract 2x from both sides to get variables all on the left side of the =.
Additive Inverse Property	$6x + 8 - 8 = -4 - 8$ $6x = -12$	Subtract 8 from both sides to get numbers all on the right side of the =.
Multiplicative Inverse Property	$\dfrac{6x}{6} = \dfrac{-12}{6}$	Divide both sides by 6 to get x by itself on the left side of the =.
Simplify	$x = -2$	Solution. Now, check your answer.
	Insert new problem	

Once you have set up your page, follow the seven steps listed below.

Step One — Record each problem step in the "Examples" section.

Step Two — Record the reasons for each step in the "Explanation" section by using abbreviations; short phrases, not sentences; key words, properties, principles or formulas.

Step Three — Record key words/concepts/rules in the left two-inch margin either during or immediately after your lecture by reworking your notes.

Step Four — Cover up the "Example and Explanation" sections and recite out loud the meaning of the key words or concepts.

Step Five — Place a check mark by the key words/concepts that you did not know.

Step Six — Review the information that you checked until it's understood.

Step Seven — Develop a math glossary for difficult-to-remember key words and concepts.

After practicing this note-taking system, you may want to modify it to meet your personal note-taking needs. Some students wait and convert their notes into a three column system after class. They also put information from the math book into the three columns. Other students use graph paper and turn it landscape in order to make the columns wider.

In some cases, auditory abstract learners do not take extensive notes. I have seen these students take down only a few notes and spend most of their working memory understanding abstract concepts. For the most part, this is fine. If you are this type of student, however, you should at least take a few notes in order to remind yourself of key concepts. You should also still develop a math glossary. It's very important for you to remember the vocabulary that connects to abstract learning. Knowing these words frees up working memory to solve difficult equations on important tests.

Creating a Math Glossary

The third component in the Seven Steps to Math Note-Taking is devoted to developing a math glossary. Since math is like a foreign language, understanding vocabulary becomes a key to learning it. A math glossary for each chapter dramatically improves learning and allows you to better remember key concepts. Your glossary can be a combination of lecture notes, text readings, or text notes.

A good glossary is a key to success for students who have good language skills but have difficulty learning math. Even though math is an abstract subject, it is still learned through using language to recall how to work problems. In fact, some students talk their way through solving equations by using their math vocabulary.

For this reason, a math glossary should be created for each chapter to define math vocabulary words and concepts. Label a section in the back of your notebook "Math Vocabulary for Chapter One." Your glossary should include all words printed in bold print in your text, words emphasized by your instructor and any other words you do not understand. If you are not sure whether or not a word is important, add it anyway just in case.

The glossary should be divided into three areas, which include the book definition, your definition in your own words, and, if appropriate, an example. When you're finished, your glossary will look similar to the note-taking system you learned about in the last section.

If you cannot explain the math vocabulary in your own words, ask your instructor or tutor for help. If your instructor or tutor cannot help you, then visit an online dictionary to find definitions. Review websites like Math.com for terms from developmental courses, and MathWords. com for terms that range from Intermediate Algebra to college Calculus. You can also, of course, simply Google a word for a direct definition.

Some students record vocabulary words with a digital recorder or smartphone. If you use a recorder or phone-app, leave a few seconds between a word and its definition. The definition should be in your own words. These vocabulary words are usually the words that you could not remember from your glossary.

To practice your vocabulary words, play the recording when you have a few minutes between classes (using headphones). This process keeps the words active in your mind until they finally pass into your long-term memory.

Once you listen to the vocabulary word, pause the recording and repeat the definition back to yourself. Replay the recording and listen to the definition. If you did not repeat it back correctly, then continue repeating it until you get it right. Keep practicing until you can correctly repeat back all the definitions. This is an excellent way for auditory math learners to memorize and learn vocabulary. Other types of learners can also use this learning system, because the repetition drills these words into your long-term memory.

Students who are visual or kinesthetic (hands on) learners may be able to learn math vocabulary more effectively by developing a virtual web-based math glossary. StudyStack. com is a free website that is designed to help people memorize and learn information.

Using the StudyStack website, you can use your computer to develop and display a stack of "virtual cards" of information that you want to learn. Just like flashcards, you can review the cards at any time, at your own pace, and you can discard the cards that you already know.

The site is set up to find information on any subject, to develop your own flashcards, to play games such as hangman

Vocabulary Card Examples	
Front	Back
Multiplicative Identity Additive Identity	Identity property a times 1 = a Additive identity a + 0 = a
Order of polynomials	Place the terms in descending order of exponents. Highest on the left to lowest on the right. x cubed, next x squared, x to the first, constant (number).
Decimals — rational numbers and irrational numbers	Rational numbers have terminating or repeating decimal equivalents. e.g. ¾ = .75, 5/7 =.714285714285… Continuing but non-repeating or nonterminating decimals are called irrational numbers (e.g. the square root of 2 and pi).

and matching, and also to help you study anytime/anywhere, 24/7. You can also print out the cards and export them to your cellphone, tablet or computer.

Visual math learners can also learn vocabulary the old fashion way — by putting a vocabulary word on one side of a flashcard and the definition on the other side. Auditory math learners can also develop flash cards, making sure to say the information out loud while learning the information.

It's also helpful to write vocabulary words next to the homework problems they are associated with. The examples above are 3x5 cards that show only words. These memory devices can be even more effective if you include pictures or other diagrams.

Taking Notes with Technology

In recent years, technological advancements have created several new resources for math students. These resources can help improve note-taking systems, accuracy, and test-reviews. They also allow you to pay more attention in the classroom in order to understand mathematical concepts, as well as record any problems you don't understand so that you can take them to your instructor or tutor at a later date. When used appropriately, technology can improve your learning and grades. However, when used inappropriately it can cause problems with your learning and instructor. This section will discuss the best ways to use note-taking technology and the pitfalls.

Smartphones

The most useful technology for modern students is perhaps the most common: your phone. In the past, students often fell behind when copying problems from the board or a PowerPoint presentation. In this case, you either had to borrow someone else's notes to fill in gaps or you simply let the gaps exist. This caused problems when reviewing notes before a test, as you couldn't remember how to get from one step to the next. Your smartphone fixes this problem.

With your instructor's permission you can use your phone to take pictures of difficult problems and even take video or audio of lectures. If your teacher highlights a particular problem type during class, for instance, you can take a picture of the whiteboard to review at a later date. This will also allow you to share these files with on-campus and off-campus tutors. This does not mean that you should avoid taking notes in class. Taking notes is still the primary way to learn new concepts. Your phone provides a backup system for note-taking, not a replacement.

Several recording applications also exist that allow you to record entire lectures. These include Smart Recorder, Voice Recorder, Evernote, and Google Docs, among others. You may already have some of these apps on your phone. If not, you can visit the appstore on your device and find these or other similar applications. Make sure to ask your instructor before using these apps in class, but, again, audio and video recordings make for a great backup resource should you fall behind during a lecture. When choosing an app, make sure to select one that allows you to mark important parts of the lecture. This way, you don't have to wait through the silence as your instructor works a problem on the board.

Another method involves only recording parts of the lecture that deal with concepts you already know you struggle with. For example, if your instructor is going over a problem that you had difficulty with on your homework, start recording. Also, don't be afraid to ask questions about the problem so that you know you are recording the exact help you'll need outside of class. Remember, the purpose of your recording is to better understand the reasons for each problem step and concept. If you don't understand a step, make sure to have your teacher clarify it.

Applications

If you are in a class that allows the use of technology, you might try any one of the following applications—all of which are available for Android and Apple devices.

Voice Recorder is a high-quality voice recording application that allow you to store your recordings as voice memos and share them with your friends. It also allows you to label recordings so you always know where to find what you're looking for.

Smart Recorder allows students to record lectures and play them back on your phone. It is designed for longer recording sessions and features a simple, user-friendly interface. Most importantly, it features an "on-the-fly" feature that automatically stops a recording during silence. This will make it easier to listen to full lectures without having to constantly fast forward.

Evernote allows students to record, amend, and take photos of notes. It also allows students to take notes by hand using one of several smart pens. It features several organizational tools that allow users to sync their notes to Microsoft Outlook and easily share these notes with peers.

Google Docs is another example of an application that allows you to take notes and save them in the Cloud. By linking a Google Doc to your Gmail, you are able to instantly save notes to the free storage included in your account. Even better, you can allow other people access the notes through their own Gmail accounts. This allows students to collaborate on a shared note file that

increases the chances that everything covered in class is available in a single file. This file is an excellent review tool to use before class, during homework sessions, or during test preparation. It also makes for an excellent agenda sheet, should you decide to hold a Skype study session with your classmates.

Smart Pens

Smart Pens are another great option for modern math students. Apple and Microsoft both offer pens for their tablets and larger phone models. These pens work well with the apps mentioned above—particularly Evernote. Students use them to write directly on the screens of the devices, most of which allow users to instantly transform hand-written notes into typed text.

Livescribe 3 Smartpen. This device requires a separate notebook, which consists of special paper that records pen motions. Users sync the pen with their tablets or smartphones through an application, which records everything they write in their notebook. Users can record audio through the tablet application, which is attached automatically to notes taken at the same time.

Summary

In this section, we have discussed several recording apps and Web-based technologies. Try out several of these applications before settling on which ones work best for you. Also, talk to your classmates to see what types of technology they use. They may have new ideas that work best for them and you.

If you are thinking about using a SmartPen, contact the Office for Students with Disabilities. This office should already have students using SmartPens and can give you suggestions or demonstrate their use. Also, ask them about the Sonocent Audio Notetaker—an app that records lectures, highlights and organizes important phrases, adds additional notes, links to your computer, and exports information. Any student can use this technology to improve note-taking.

How to Rework Your Notes

A good note-taking system does not stop when you leave the classroom. As soon as possible after class, rework your notes to decrease the chances you will forget something important. This is an excellent procedure to transfer math information from short-term to long-term memory and abstract reasoning.

Remember: Most forgetting occurs right after learning material. You need to rework your notes as soon as possible. The longer you wait, the more you forget and have to relearn.

1. *Rewrite the material you cannot read or will not be able to understand a few weeks later.* If you do not rework your notes, you will become frustrated when you come across illegible writing while studying for a test. Another benefit of rewriting your notes is that you immediately learn new material. Waiting means it will take more time to learn material.

2. *Fill in the gaps.* Most of the time, when you are listening to a lecture, you cannot write down everything. Locate the portions of your notes, which are incomplete. Fill in the concepts that were left out. In the future, skip two or three lines in your notebook page for anticipated lecture gaps.

3. *Add additional key words and ideas in the left-hand column.* These key words or ideas were the ones not recorded during the lecture. Example: You did not know you should add the opposite of 18 to solve a particular problem, and you incorrectly added 18. Put additional important key words and ideas (such as "opposite"and "negative of") in the notes; these are the words that will improve your understanding of math.

4. *Add to your problem log the problems which the teacher worked in class.* The problem log is a separate section of your notebook that contains a listing of problems (without explanations — just problems) your teacher worked in class. If your teacher chose those problems to work in class, you can bet that they are considered important. The problems in this log can be used as a practice test for the next exam. Your regular class notes will not only contain the solutions but also all the steps involved in arriving at those solutions. These notes can be used as a reference when you take your practice test. This process prepares you for exams by giving you a basic feel for potential test questions.

5. *Add calculator keystroke sequences to your calculator handbook.* The calculator handbook can be a spiral-bound set of notecards or a separate section of your notebook that holds only calculator-related information. Your handbook should also include an explanation of when that particular set of keystrokes is to be used.

6. *Reflection and synthesis.* Once you have finished going over your notes, review the major points in your mind. Combine your new notes with your previous knowledge to have a better understanding of what you've learned today.

Additional Strategies to Use Audio Recordings While Taking Notes

If you have problems recording information in your math class, first ask your instructor about recording the lecture. To ensure success, the recorder or phone application must have a counter and must be voice activated. This way, you can start and stop during lectures while also keeping track of when a particular piece of information was mentioned.

Most recording applications display a sliding time bar, which allows you to know exactly where you are in a lecture. When you find you're in an area of confusing information while you're recording the lecture, write down the beginning and ending times in the left margin of your notes. When reviewing your notes, the counter number is a reference point for obtaining information to work the problem. Also, reduce the time it takes to listen to the recording by using the pause button to stop it while your professor covers unnecessary material during a lecture.

Most smartphone applications also contain valuable organization and time-saving tools. Remember, however, that you must always ask permission before using your smartphone in class.

Additional Strategies to Ask Questions

To get the most out of a lecture, you must ask questions in class. By asking questions, you improve your understanding of material and decrease your homework time. By not asking questions, you create unnecessary confusion during the remainder of a class period.

Also, it is much easier to ask questions in class about potential homework problems than it is to spend hours trying to figure out the problems on your own.

If you are shy about asking questions in class, write down any questions you may have and read them to your instructor. If the instructor seems confused about the questions, tell him or her that you will discuss the problem after class. Most professors are more than willing to help you during the moments immediately following a lecture.

Another trick is to prepare a question before class. This question can be something you are confused about, or something you already know. By forcing yourself to ask a question—any question—at the onset of a lecture, you can alleviate any nervousness you may have about asking questions in the future.

To encourage yourself to ask questions, remember:

- You have paid for your instructor's help.
- Other students probably have the same or similar questions.
- The instructor needs feedback on his or her teaching to help the class learn material.
- Not asking a question can stop your learning.
- There is no such thing as a "stupid" question.
- Asking questions during class lets a professor know you are interested in his or her lecture. Engaging a teacher during class makes it much more likely they will help you when you get confused.

How to Take Notes for Online and Computer-Based Instruction

Modern math students have more course options than any generation in collegiate history. Two of the newest options, online courses and computer-based instruction courses, differ from classes held in traditional math classrooms.

Online distance courses allow students to use course software to complete a class outside of the classroom. Students are required to finish a pre-set curriculum by a certain date, though they are mostly left to complete the work where and when the want.

Computer-based instruction courses, on the other hand, are taken in specified classrooms on specified dates. These courses, often held in computer labs, do not typically include lectures, nor do they require students to work at a specific pace. These courses often use similar software to that used in online distance courses, though students typically benefit from having a professor or a group of tutors in the room to answer their questions.

Because there are no planned lectures, most computer-based learning students dive immediately into their homework without taking any notes — this despite the fact that most math software programs allow students to easily find specific passages from the required textbook and even provide extremely detailed, video-based walkthroughs. Having observed many of these classes, however, I've noticed most students prefer to rely on built-in support buttons, which answer their questions as they progress through their assignments. This practice — also common among online distance learners — is extremely dangerous. While these support buttons are often helpful, they are intended to provide reminders, not to take the place of proper lectures.

Just because you're allowed to move at your own pace does not mean that you should skip lectures and move directly to assignments. If you want to succeed in your online or computer-based course, you must treat it exactly the same way you would a traditional course. This means that you must read the text and take copious, detailed notes.

With this in mind, online and computer-based courses require their own, unique note-taking system. Traditional classroom notes are mainly taken to help you complete your homework assignments. Computer-based notes are taken to help you review for online quizzes and tests. This means that it's more important than ever to remember every step to every type of problem.

Note-Taking Memory Cues and Steps

The first thing you should notice about this note-taking system is that it looks similar to the "Seven Steps to Math Note-Taking" system given in the previous unit. Any similarities between the two systems are all cosmetic. The memory cues and problems steps are much different on computers.

Using this system enhances your math learning as you complete new units in your software. It also provides you with a set of comprehensive study guides for quizzes and tests. Students can use this note-taking system in two different formats. Some students will use it while doing their homework. Other students will use their regular note-taking system and then transfer their notes into this system after class. I prefer that you use the first way because it will save you time in the long run; however, if you do not have access to the Internet at home, you may have to use the second system and rework your notes when you get back from class. If this is the case for you, you may want to print out or write down the problem steps you find through the "Help" and "Example" buttons in your software. This way you won't be at a disadvantage come test day.

When taking notes in an online or computer-based course, you should focus on any problem that you had to attempt two or three times. Also, focus on any problems on which you required help from your professor, lab assistant, or online tutoring program.

Setting up Your Notebook Page

Before you take any notes, you first need to label the top of your notebook page with the homework section and problem numbers the notes refer to. Also, include the date on which

you are working on these problems. Once you've done this, complete the following steps:

1. *Label the top* space between the notebook ring and the red line, "Key Words."
2. *Label the other* side of the red line, "Examples."
3. *In the spot* to the right of "Examples," label a third section "Explanations/Rules."
4. *Draw vertical lines* on each side of the "Examples" section. By doing so, you are setting up three different columns.
5. *Record the same* information on the next 10 pages of your notebook. After using this system for 10 pages, you may not need to label each page.

Seven Steps to Taking Computer-based Instruction Notes

Once you've set up your page, follow the seven steps listed below:

Step One — Record a problem and each of its steps in the "Examples" section.

Step Two — Record the reasons for each step in the "Explanation" section by using abbreviations; short phrases, not sentences; keywords, properties, principles or formulas. If you do not know the explanations for a particular step, click on your "Help Me Solve This" or "Example" button. Condense this information in a sentence or two above or below the problem. If you do not understand the phrases you find in the help sections, click on the "Textbook Help" button and locate the definitions of any words you don't know. If you still have difficulty, click on the "Video" button or ask your instructor or tutor for help.

Step Three — Record key words and rules in the left two-inch margin either during or immediately after an online lecture by reworking your notes. If you're in the middle of an assignment, find these words at the right of each step in the "Help Me Solve" and "Examples" sections.

Step Four — Cover up the "Example and Explanation" sections and recite out loud the meaning of the key words or concepts.

Step Five — Place a check mark by the key words/concepts that you did not know.

Step Six — Review the information that you checked until it is understood.

Step Seven — Develop a math glossary for difficult-to-remember key words and concepts.

When you finish, your notes should look like the notecard printed on the next page. After practicing this system, you may want to modify it to write down only the explanations that you do not understand or feel you might forget. As mentioned earlier, some students wait to convert their notes into a three column system until after class. This is perfectly fine. The key is to organize the details in your notes into a system that connects problem steps with the reasons the steps are necessary.

The Importance of Emailing Your Teachers

Students taking online courses especially need to develop and use this note-taking system. Online students do not have the luxury of taking notes while asking a tutor or instructor to help them solve the problems. Online students must depend more on "Help" and "Example" buttons. If these buttons don't help you understand how to solve a problem, you need to take notes from the support videos and textbook.

Taking all these notes may be time consuming; however, you need to put the information in your own words in order to better understand the concept.

The next logical question is, "What do I do if after taking the notes from various resources, I still don't understand how to solve the problem?"

The answer is very obvious but according to many online instructors most students don't do it. *Email your instructor and ask about how to solve difficult problems.* That is not to say that the instructors don't get emails from students. The emails they do get are usually technical questions about accessing or operating online homework. Many math instructors wish the questions were about solving homework problems.

Emailing math instructors to help you solve homework problems is similar to using the listening skills we discussed earlier in this chapter. Don't email the instructor the problem just to indicate that you cannot do the problem; send the problem along with your attempted problem steps, and indicate where you got stuck. After the instructor helps you solve the problems, take notes on the steps.

Next, ask the instructor to guide you to online resources for solving similar problems. Check those resources to see if you did review them or if they are new resources.

If you email your instructor a question about a problem, you will probably make his or her day. Conversely, the Instructional Technology team at your college loves to answer technological problems. Direct to them any and all such inquires.

If you are in the emporium model, don't be afraid to ask your instructor or tutor to help you with notes. Most students have difficulty filling in "Explanation" sections. Have the tutor or instructor explain the reasons for a problem's steps. Don't, however, write down their explanation. Rephrase the explanation into your own words, and ask them if this is what they meant. Then write down your explanation because you remember your own words better while taking tests. This translation helps transfer math concepts into long-term memory and abstract reasoning.

Computer-Based Instruction/Online Three-Column Note-Taking Method

Key Words and Rules	Examples	Explanations
Words from the right side of problem	The problem	Sentences that describe the next step or sentences at the end of the problem
Solve a linear equation.	$5(x + 4) + 3(x - 4) = 2(x - 2)$	Get x on one side of the = sign and a number on the on the other side
Distributive Property	$5x + 20 + 3x - 12 = 2x - 4$	Use the distributive property: multiply number outside () by the variable and number
Add like terms	$8x + 8 = 2x - 4$	Add numbers and like variables
Additive Inverse	$8x - 2x + 8 = 2x - 2x - 4$	Get numbers on one side
Subtract like terms	$6x + 8 = -4$	Get the variable on one side.
Additive Inverse	$6x + 8 - 8 = -4 - 8$	Get the x on one side and the number on the other
Simplify	$6x = -12$	Simplify the equation.
Multiplicative Inverse	$\dfrac{6x}{6} = \dfrac{-12}{6}$	Divide by 6 to get x
Simplify	$x = -2$	Solution. Does it make sense?

Chapter Two: Checklist for Knowledge and Behaviors

Put a check after understanding the knowledge statements and fill in the behavioral activities.

Chapter Knowledge

1. I understand that effective listening is the first step to excellent note-taking. _____

2. I know that the goal of note-taking is to write the least amount possible to record the most information. _____

3. I know my instructor's cues for writing down important information. _____

4. I understand that the Modified Three-Column Note-Taking Example is an excellent example to use for both taking notes and testing myself on information. I cover up the left side of the note page and recall the information, then study the information I did not recall. _____

5. I know to write down everything the instructor writes on the board or PowerPoint-slides. _____

6. I know that asking questions in math class can decrease my homework time. _____

7. I know that using note-taking technology can help improve my note-taking skills and learning. _____.

8. I know that if I wait too long to review my notes, I may not understand them later. This makes it more difficult to learn. _____

9. I know that online and computer-based-learning students need to use a special note-taking system, which differs in many ways from traditional note-taking systems. _____

10. I know that online and computer-based learning courses require more independent learning and motivation. _____

Behavioral Activities

1. I show up to class at least a few minutes early to "warm up" to take notes. _____

2. I always bring my notebook, textbook, and calculator to class._____

3. I sit in the front or middle of the classroom and practice good listening techniques. ___

4. I ask questions about anything that is not clear. _____

5. I only use my smartphone when the instructor allows me to record information or take pictures of the board. _____

6. I review my notes right after class and fill in what I missed. _____

7. I compare my notes with a classmate before the next class. _____

8. I have developed a math glossary to help me understand math vocabulary. _____

9. I visit my instructor to review the classroom notes I don't understand. _____

10. I email my instructor about concepts or problems I don't understand. _____

Name: _____   Date: _____

Assignment for Chapter 2

Answer the following questions on a separate sheet of paper.

1. Review and use the Modified Three-Column Note-Taking figure as a model for your notes. List and define the key words that were discussed while using this system:

2. What are two reasons for warming up for a math class?

3. List and explain three strategies to help you become an active listener.

4. Describe the listening and questioning skills you need to communicate with your instructor when visiting his or her office.

5. List the reasons you need to copy down each step of every math problem.

6. List and explain three ways a math glossary can improve math learning.

7. How is the note-taking system for online or computer-based learning different than classroom notes?

8. Describe three note-taking technology strategies that you use to improve note-taking.

9. Describe the overall purpose for taking classroom, computer-based learning, or online-class notes as it relates to homework, learning, and passing tests.

10. List and explain the Seven Steps to Math Note Taking. If you are taking an online or computer-based class, list the Seven Steps to Taking Online Math Notes instead.

How to Improve Study Environment, Time Management, and Reading

In Chapter 3
You will learn these concepts:

- ✓ How to develop a detailed study schedule
- ✓ How to design an effective study environment
- ✓ When to read your textbook
- ✓ How to effectively read your math textbook
- ✓ How to effectively read an online textbook or chapter

Setting up an Effective Study Environment

While most students understand the importance of recognizing *what* to study, many do not understand that *where* you study plays a huge role in how you do in a math course. A positive home and college study environment improves your learning experiences.

Traditional study environments include on-campus study areas, such as libraries and reading rooms, and off-campus study areas, like your house or a coffee shop. Today's students, however, have many additional options. Other study environments include math labs, Learning Resource Centers (LRC), study groups, Supplemental Instruction, collaborative learning programs and websites. These new environments require students to learn how to use resources in the math lab/ LRC such as: computer programs, homework software and assessment instruments.

The learning environment in the classroom has also changed, and it now emphasizes more collaborative learning. Students now have to learn how to benefit from their collaborative classroom learning experiences and how to make the best use of the math lab or LRC. Learning outside the classroom has also changed. Students need to learn how to effectively use collaborative learning, study groups and Supplemental Instruction. To maximize learning, students need to effectively use their new study environments and learning resources.

Another way to maximize learning is to effectively manage your time. In high school, teachers and parents often manage a student's time. In college, students suddenly have more activities (work, social, study) and less time to fit them all in (and no teachers or parents handy or willing to schedule their time for them). When freshman college students are asked to give their number one reason for poor grades, they indicate that they do not have enough time to study. When students are asked how much time they study per week, most do not have any idea.

Students who do not effectively manage their study time may fail math courses. As pointed out in Chapter 1, math requires much practice (the same as mastering a sport or musical instrument) for the student to perform well on tests. Therefore, developing a good plan for studying math is key to getting good grades.

Choosing a Place to Study

Choosing a place to study is tricky business. Some study environments have too many distractions. Other study environments may be quiet, but do not have the necessary materials around to supplement your work.

For as long as students have attended college, this quandary has caused indecision and frustration. In some ways, however, modern math students have it worse than any previous generation. Thanks to laptops, tablets and smartphones, you can study anytime and anywhere, so long as you have the right attitude and a fully charged battery. This sounds like a good thing, but with an excess of options, many students become overwhelmed. As the old saying goes, the grass is always greener. With so many viable places to study, how can you be certain to choose the ideal location?

The answer to this question is deceptively simple. As long as you choose a place that suits your particular needs and establish a routine that automatically puts you in the right state of mind, you really can't go wrong.

Wherever you study, the key is to develop working familiarity with your study area. While studying in your home, choose one place, one chair, one desk or table. If you use the kitchen table, choose one chair, preferably one that you do not use during dinner. Call this chair "my study chair." If you study in the student cafeteria, use the same table each time. Do not use the table at which you play cards, video games or eat. By studying at the same place each time, you form a conditioned response. From then on, when you sit down at your study place your mind will automatically start thinking about studying. This conditioned response decreases your "warm up" time. "Warm up" time is how long it takes to actually begin studying after you sit down. Another aspect of the study environment involves the degree of silence you need for studying. In most cases, a totally quiet room is not necessary. But if you can only study with total silence, keep this in mind when selecting your study places.

Most students can study with a little noise, especially if it is constant, like music from their MP3 players or phones. In fact, some students keep on a mellow radio station or a fan to drown out other noises. However, do not turn on the television to drown out other noises while studying. That will not work! Why? Because you are likely to get distracted. Always select a study area where you can control the noise level.

All Study Areas Should Have:

1. The tools of your trade: pencils, paper, calculator, phone, tablet, computer, etc

2. A copy of your study schedule

3. Images that will reinforce your goals: pictures of people in your desired profession, images of potential rewards for your hard work, etc

4. If you need background noise, you should bring your phone to play ambient music or sound

5. Once you sit down, avoid getting back up, so bring light snacks and water if you think you might get hungry

Setting up Your Study Area

If you decide to study at home, signs should surround your environment that "tell" you to study. This includes a copy of your study schedule. Attach your study schedule to the inside flap of your notebook and place another copy where you study at home. It is also okay to put your schedule on your cellphone. Place your study goals and the rewards for achieving those goals where they are easily seen. Do not post pictures of your girlfriend, boyfriend or other distracting items in your study area. Instead, post pictures indicating your goals after graduation. If you want to be a nurse, doctor, or business person, post pictures that represent these goals. Your study area should always reinforce your educational goals.

When sitting down to study, have ready the "tools of your trade": pencils, paper, a notebook, a textbook, a study guide, phone, tablet, calculator, etc. Everything should be well within reach. This way, when you need something, you don't have to leave your study area. The problem with getting up is not just the time it takes to get the item, but the time it takes to "warm up" again. After getting milk and cookies and sitting down, it takes another four to five minutes to "warm up" and continue studying.

The Best Way to Study Subjects

When studying, arrange your subjects in the order of difficulty. In other words, start with your most difficult subject — which is usually math — and work toward your easiest course. By studying your most difficult subject first, you are more alert and better motivated to complete the work before continuing on the easier courses, which may be more interesting to you. If you study math last, you will probably tire easily, become frustrated and quit; however, you are less likely to quit when you study a subject that interests you.

Change the Order of Study

Another approach to improving the quality of your study is to mix up the order of studying different subjects.

Example: If you have English, accounting and math to study, then study them in the following order: 1. math, 2. English, and 3. accounting. By studying the subjects in this order, one part of your brain can rest after studying math while the other part of your brain is studying English. Now your mind is "fresh" when you study accounting.

The key to this strategy is to study your easier subjects between your harder subjects. Obviously, the terms "easy" and "hard" are subjective, so you need to personalize this strategy based upon your own skills and interests. If English comes easy to you, use it as a buffer between more troublesome subjects. Not only does this strategy allow your mind rest, but it also keeps you in good spirits. The frustration that builds during difficult math study sessions is quickly forgotten after a successful bout with your favorite subject.

Deciding When to Study

Deciding when to study different types of material is also part of developing a positive study environment. Your study material can be divided into two separate types: new material and material that has already been learned. The best time to review material you've already learned is right before going to sleep. By reviewing material for the test the night before, you have less brain activity and fewer physical distractions that prevent you from recalling important material the next day.

Example: If you have an 8:00 test the next morning, you should review the material the night before. If you have a 10:00 test the next day, review the material both the night before and the day of the test. Reviewing is defined as reading the material to yourself. You also might review a few problems you have already solved to keep your mind alert, but do not try to learn any new material the night before the test.

When to Learn New Material

Learning new material should be done during the first part of the study period. Do not learn new material the night before a test. You will be setting yourself up for test anxiety. If you try to cram the procedures to solve different types of equations or new ways to factor trinomials, you will end up in a state of confusion. This is especially true if you have major problems learning how to solve new equations or factoring. The next day you will only remember not being able to solve the equation or factor the trinomials; this could distract you on the test.

Most students get tired after studying for several hours or before going to bed. If you are tired and try to study new material, it becomes more difficult to retain. It takes more effort to learn new material when you are tired than it does to review old material. When you start getting tired of studying, the best tactic is to begin reviewing previously learned material. This way, your brain stays in work mode while your body adjusts to your waning energy levels.

Find the Most Efficient Time to Study Math

The most efficient time to study is as soon as possible after the math class is over. Psychologists indicate that most forgetting occurs right after learning the material. In other words, you are going to forget most of what you have learned in the first hour after class. To prevent this mass exodus of knowledge, you need to recall some of the lecture material as soon after class as is practical.

The easiest way to recall the lecture is to rework your notes. Reviewing your notes will increase your ability to recall the information and make it easier to understand the homework assignments. We covered this topic extensively in Chapter Two—where you learned how to turn a set of sloppy notes into a well-organized study tool. If necessary, review this information.

Choosing Between Mass and Distributive Learning

There are two different types of learning processes: "mass learning" and "distributive learning." Mass learning involves learning everything at one time. Distributive learning is studying the same amount of time as mass learning with the addition of several study breaks. In the past, many educators preached mass learning above all else. Now, however, most teach their students to take frequent breaks.

> Example: Mass learning—you would study three hours in a row without taking a break, then quit studying for the night. Distributive learning — you would study for about 50 minutes with a 10 minute break, study for 50 more minutes with a 10 minute break, and finish with 60 minutes of studying before stopping.

Benefits of Study Breaks

Psychologists have discovered that learning decreases if you do not take study breaks. Therefore, use the distributive learning procedures (described above) to study math. Study breaks keep you from becoming overly frustrated with your studies. In this way, taking regular study breaks allows you to study for longer intervals.

If you continue to force yourself to study, you will not learn the material. After taking a break, return to studying. If you still cannot study after taking a break, review your purpose for studying and your educational goals.

Think about what is required to graduate; it will probably come down to the fact that you have to pass math. Studying math today will help you pass the next test; this increases your chances of passing the course and eventually graduating. If this does not motivate you to stick with your studies, nothing will.

How to Develop a Study Schedule

Before starting to develop a study schedule, let's look at studying and learning effectiveness based on educational psychology. Educational psychologists have conducted research on studying and memory and found out the best time to study is right after class. Research shows that most students lose up to 50% of the information learned in class by the next day. The closer you can schedule doing homework, reviewing your notes or reading your textbook after class, the more likely you'll retain information.

If possible, when working out your schedule, reserve a one or two hour space right after class for studying. If you have back-to-back classes, then schedule study time for as soon as possible after your last class. Even if your schedule has very few breaks, spend at least a few minutes reviewing your notes the same day. Remember, studying right after class is the best way to learn.

Educational psychologists have also conducted research to see what students remember most clearly the next day after studying several subjects. Research indicates that the subject you studied last is what you remember best the next day. This means that you should review your most challenging subject before going to bed each night. This is especially true the night before a test.

Biological Clock

Research also shows that your biological clock has a significant impact on your ability to develop study habits. Most of us learn best at different times of the day.

Try to schedule your study times to match your daily biological clock. If you are a morning person, then don't schedule your study time for late at night. If you are a late-night person, then don't schedule your study time for early in the morning. It will take about two weeks to develop this new schedule into a habit. Once you have, your body and your mind should sync up, giving you the best chance to retain information.

Schedule Weekly Study Time

Now let's look at how you can develop a study schedule while keeping these important points in mind. There are two basic reasons for developing a study schedule: To schedule your study time and to become more efficient at studying. Before moving on, complete Activity 3.1. This way you will know how you are currently scheduling your time.

In order to become a more efficient studier, you need to set aside a certain amount of study time each week. Rather than setting up a number of daily study hours, you should focus on the number of hours, per week, you plan to devote to studying. How many hours do you study per week? Ten hours, 15 hours, 20 hours, 30 hours? Without knowing the amount of your study hours per week, you will not know if you are studying at a productive rate. Many students believe they are studying enough to make their desired grade, when in truth, they are coming up drastically short.

> Example: If your goal is to make a B average, and with studying 15 hours per week you make all B's on your tests, then the goal has been met. However, if you study 15 hours per week and make all D's, then you need to increase your study time and/or change your study methods. By monitoring your grades and the number of hours you study per week, you can adjust your study schedule to get the grades you want.

By monitoring your grades and the number of hours you study per week, you can adjust your study schedule accordingly.

> Example: You are shopping online or playing video games on a Sunday afternoon, when you start feeling guilty." You have not started studying for that math test on Monday. If you had created a study schedule, you could have arranged to study for the math test on Saturday and still have been able to enjoy shopping or football on Sunday.

The second reason for developing a study schedule is to use time more efficiently. Efficient study means knowing when you are supposed to study and when you do not have to study. This approach will help keep you from thinking about other things you should be doing when you sit down to study. The reverse is also true. When doing other, more enjoyable things, you will not feel guilty about not studying.

A study schedule should be set up for two reasons: To determine the amount of study time you need, per week, to get the grades you want and to set up peak efficient study times.

How to Prioritize Your Time

To develop a study schedule, review the Planning Use of Daily Time chart printed on page 67. Use the chart to map out planned study times—feel free to make enlarged copies if you wish.

The best way to begin to develop your study schedule is to fill in all the times you cannot study. Do this by following the steps printed on the next few pages. Some of these steps may not apply to you. If so, replace the step with something unique to your schedule.

1. *Fill in all your classes by putting code C.* For example, if you have an 8:00-9:30 class, draw a line through the center of the 9:00 a.m. box on the study schedule.

2. *Fill in the time you work with code W (W = work).* This may be difficult, since some students' work schedules may change during the week. The best way to predict work time is to base it on the time you worked the previous week, unless you are on a rotating shift. Indicate your approximate work times on the study schedule. As your work hours change, revise the study schedule. Remember: Your study schedule should be structured around the number of hours a week you plan to study. Realize that while your work times might change every week, your total weekly work hours usually remain the same.

3. *Decide the amount of time it takes to eat (E = eat) breakfast, lunch and dinner.* This time slot should include both food preparation and clean up. Keep in mind that the amount of time it takes to eat may fluctuate. Eating time also includes time spent in the student cafeteria. If you have an 11:00-12:00 or 1:00-2:00 lunch break, you

might not eat during the entire time; you could be there both socializing and eating. Still put code E in the study schedule, since the main use of your time is for eating.

4. *Include your grooming time (G = grooming).* Some grooming activities include taking a bath, washing your hair or other activities that you do to get ready for school, dates or work. Grooming varies from minutes to hours per day for college students. Mark your study schedule with code G for the usual amount of time spent on grooming. Remember that more time might be spent on grooming during weekends.

5. *Include your tutor time (T = tutor).* This is not considered study time. Tutor time is strictly that which you spend in a tutoring session. If you have a tutor scheduled or meet weekly with your instructor, mark these times with code T in the study schedule.

6. *Reserve time for family responsibilities on the study schedule (F = family responsibilities).* Some family responsibilities include taking your child on errands, mowing the lawn, grocery shopping and taking out the garbage. Also, if you have arranged to take your children some place every Saturday morning, then put it on the study schedule using code F.

7. *Figure out how much time is spent on cleaning each week (CN = cleaning).* This time can include cleaning your dorm room, house, car, and clothes. Cleaning time usually takes several hours a week. Indicate with code CN that you have cleaning time on the study schedule, and make sure it is adequate for the entire week.

8. *Review your sleep patterns for the week (SL = sleep).* Your sleep time will probably be the same from Monday through Friday. On the weekend, you might sleep later during the day and stay up later at night. Be realistic when scheduling your sleep time. If you have been sleeping on Saturday mornings until 10:00 a.m. for the last two or three years, do not plan time at 8:00 a.m. to study.

9. *Figure the amount of weekly social time (SC = social time).* Social time includes being with other people, watching TV, or being on Instagram. It can be doing nothing at all or going out and having a good time. You need to have some social time during the week or you will burn out, and you will probably drop out of school. You may last only one semester. If you study and work too hard without some relaxation, you will not last the entire school year. Some daily social time is needed, but do not overdo it.

10. *Figure the amount of travel time to and from work (TR= travel time).* Travel time could be driving to and from college or riding the subway. If possible, use travel to listen to recordings of your class or to review notes. Travel time may vary during different times of the year.

11. *Recall other time obligations that have not been previously mentioned (O = other).* Other time obligations may be aspects of your life, which you do not want to share with other people. Review the study schedule for any other time obligations and mark them.

Once you have finished all of the steps, count up all the blank spaces. Each blank space represents one hour. You might have several half-blank spaces, which each represent one-half hour. Add together the number of blank spaces left and write the total in the oval, which is located on the lower right-hand corner of the study schedule.

Next, figure how many hours you have to study during the week. The rule of thumb is to study approximately two hours per week for each class hour. If you have 12 real class hours per week, you should be studying 20-24 hours per week to make A's and B's. Write the amount of time you want to study per week in the square, located in the lower left-hand corner of your study schedule. This is a study "contract" you are making with yourself.

If the number of contracted (square) study hours is less than the number in the oval, then fill in the times you want to study (S = study). First, fill in the best times to study. If there are unmarked spaces, use them as backup study time. Now you have a schedule of the best times to study. On the other hand, if you want to study 15 hours a week and have only 10 hours of space, you have to make a decision. Go back over your study-schedule codes and locate where you can change some times.

If you have a problem locating additional study time, make a priority time list. Take the hours away from the items with the least priority. Complete the study schedule by putting in your best study times. Also, feel free to use one of the many computer-based, phone-based and tablet-based software applications that send you notifications about important events or due dates.

These programs, which usually come pre-installed, send you text messages or emails to make sure you don't miss important points on your schedule.

How to Choose the Grade You Want

Determine what grade you want to make in the math course and write the grade on the study schedule. The grade should be an A, a B or a C. Do not write an N, W, X or F because these grades mean you will not successfully complete the course. Do not write D because you may not get credit for the course or be allowed to take the next course. In fact, it is not wise to write C, either, because most students who make a C usually fail their next algebra course. Your selected grade is now your goal.

Currently, you have a study schedule representing the number of hours of study per week. You also have a course grade goal. After you have been in the course for several weeks and get back the results of your first tests, you will know if you are accomplishing your goal. Should you not meet your goal, improve the quality and quantity of your studying or lower your course grade goal.

How to Create a Weekly Study Plan

By using the information from your completed copy of the Planning Use of Daily Time chart, you will know which time slots are available for study. You can use this information to both develop an effective study plan for the next week and establish weekly study goals.

Each Sunday, use a sheet of paper to record the days of the week from Monday to Sunday. Label it as your Weekly Study Plan and indicate the best days to study each subject. Give first priority to the best times to study math. Therefore you should choose study times that are as close to class time as possible. Be sure to indicate where you will study. Are you going to go to the math lab? Are you going to study in a group at someone's home or workplace? Are you going to study alone at the library?

Once you have indicated in the Weekly Study Goal Sheet your math study times and locations, fill in your study goals for other subjects. If your math class is the last class of the day, schedule your math study time in the first study-time slot. Therefore, you would choose to begin studying your daily math at 3:00 on Monday, Tuesday, Wednesday and Thursday. You will mark the box on the math line for Monday, Tuesday, Wednesday and Thursday with: 3 p.m., daily work, home.

How to Manage
Work and Study Schedules

Most college students work and attend college at the same time. Some college students even try to be full-time students and employees. This can be dangerous because many full-time college students who attempt to work full time wind up dropping out. Students who work and attend college at the same time must manage their time very carefully and balance their work and study schedules.

Students can be successful in college while working; however, it takes effective time management along with excellent reading and study techniques. Make sure you are not setting yourself up to be successful at work while failing college. If necessary, drop to part-time work while in college and work overtime to obtain enough money to attend college. Also, it is better to "stop out" of college for a term and work instead of juggling both. This is especially true if your work is causing you to fail classes. However, you should only "stop out" for one semester because many students who stay out of college more than one semester don't come back. The suggestions below can help you best manage work and study:

- Try to find a job that allows you some opportunity to study.

- Try to arrange to work right after class. Do not go home first. Take work clothes with you to school if needed.

- Try to review your notes during work if the job allows.

- Record class lectures and play them during your travel to and from work.

- Take only 12 semester hours,which will qualify you as full-time for financial aid but will not over-burden your time.

- Do not wait until the weekend to do your homework.

- During breaks or lunch review your notes or use apps to practice/review math.

Another way to help manage your study schedule and work is to take online courses. Some students set up on campus courses on M, W, F and their work schedules for T, TH, and weekends. They take one or two online courses so they do not have to drive to college and can work on the courses at night. This saves travel time; however, there is more demand for time management. You have to set up the same time each day for online courses. This makes more time for studying and working, but causes major problems if you get behind in your coursework.

I recommend taking social science courses such as Psychology, History, or Sociology online. These courses are not sequential in nature, so if you do get behind you can catch up quickly. I do not recommend math or STEM courses unless you are very good at them. As you learned in Chapter One, getting behind in math can cause failure.

If you are short on time and still need to work, you may want to ask about working at your college through the College Work Study program. This program is federally funded and is based on financial need. The college does not pay you. The money comes from the federal government. If you do not qualify for College Work Study, you may still be able to work on campus through department funds; for example, at the library or at a food services location. These funds come directly from the college or department based on their budget. The downside is that colleges tend to pay lower wages than outside employers. However, colleges work with your schedule and there is no driving time or gas money involved. I have had many students work for me as tutors or study coaches up to 25 hours a week, and they thought it was a good opportunity. See if working at your college is a good option for you.

Summary

When planned, managing work and studying is possible, although it requires innovative uses of your time. You may need to let your co-workers know that you are going to college and need to occasionally study during breaks. You must also adhere to your study schedule outside of work to be most effective. However, you still have to have some fun social time, and, if you have a family, some family time. This will keep your spirits up, even as you manage your busy schedule.

Planning Use of Daily Time

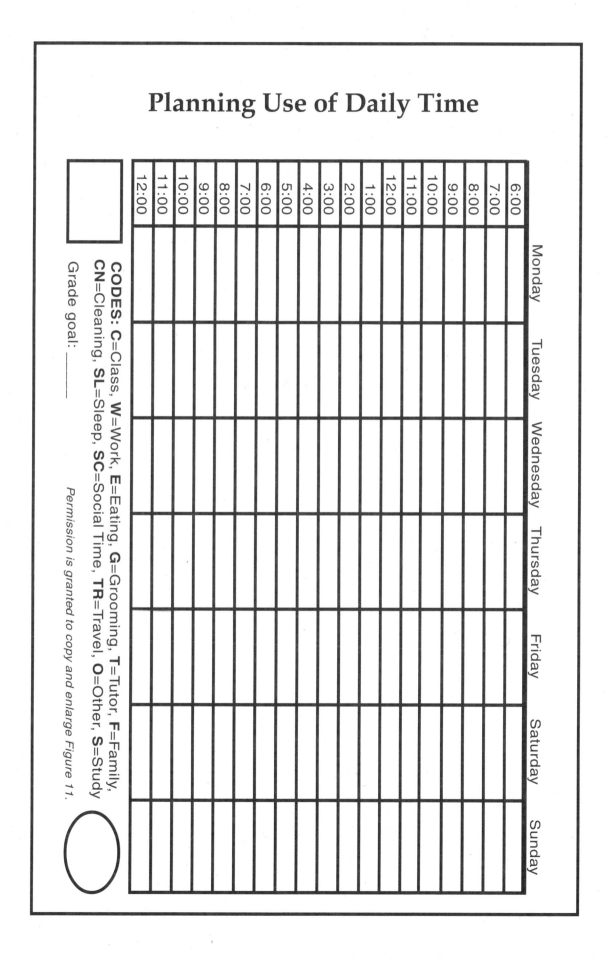

	Monday	Tuesday	Wednesday	Thursday	Friday	Saturday	Sunday
6:00							
7:00							
8:00							
9:00							
10:00							
11:00							
12:00							
1:00							
2:00							
3:00							
4:00							
5:00							
6:00							
7:00							
8:00							
9:00							
10:00							
11:00							
12:00							

CODES: C=Class, **W**=Work, **E**=Eating, **G**=Grooming, **T**=Tutor, **F**=Family, **CN**=Cleaning, **SL**=Sleep, **SC**=Social Time, **TR**=Travel, **O**=Other, **S**=Study

Grade goal: _____

Permission is granted to copy and enlarge Figure 11.

Activity 3.1 Assessing Time Management

Before filling out your study schedule, we need to access your current status of time management, your GPA, and your math grade goals. Complete this short self-assessment to obtain your current status. You may have to guess at some of the questions. This is OK.

1. In the space below, list the GPA your want to have this semester, as well as the reasons you want to achieve this GPA.

GPA _____
Reasons:

2. In the space below, select the math grade you want to achieve, as well as the reasons you want this particular grade.

Math grade _____
Reasons:

3. In the space below, write down the grade you made on your last math test. If you have not had a test yet, list your last math course grade.

Math test grade or last math course grade_____

4. In the space below, list how many hours you spend in tutoring either at a math lab or a learning resource center, then write down whether or not you believe this is enough time to achieve the grade you want.

Hours a week in math lab/LRC _____
Explain:

5. In the space below, list the amount of hours you spend studying math every week, as well as your total study hours (for all of your courses). Is this enough time to achieve the GPA you want to obtain? If not, what will you do differently?
Math study hours _____
Total study hours _____
Explain:

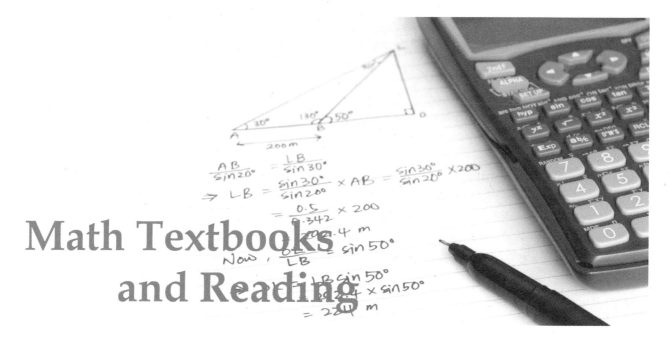

Math Textbooks and Reading

Knowing how to read a math textbook and complete homework is vital to succeeding in mathematics. Understanding and retaining material from your text makes it much more likely that you will follow lectures and succeed on tests. While this is true in all college courses, having the skill set to read and digest information from a text is more important in math than perhaps any other subject.

Unfortunately, many students struggle with math textbooks, which are far more technical and harder to follow than those used in other courses. Worse, because math instructors know how to read and learn from these books, they often assume that students are capable of figuring out how to solve math problems through assigned readings. The truth is, most students are never taught how to read a math text. This disconnect is at the heart of many students' struggles with the subject.

It is not enough to merely dive into a math textbook. You must develop a system. The same is also true of homework. Most math students do not have a homework system. They begin their homework by going directly to the problems and trying to work them. When they get stuck, they quit. This is not a good homework system. A good system improves success in homework. It also helps

your overall understanding of math. Two key components to a good study system deal with using the textbook as a resource and completing homework to learn math well enough to perform during a timed test (see next chapter). This chapter helps you design a system that allows you to learn from your math textbook and use it as an invaluable resource for completing homework.

It's also worth noting that more and more math classes are either being taught online or through the computer-based learning model. These courses require students to read online textbooks and complete online homework problems. Reading online texts requires a new set of reading skills that most students don't have.

In most cases, students don't read the online text or section of the text that is paired with homework problems. They see no value in reading this material. Also, most students start doing homework without a plan. After several tries, they may get a few problems correct, but they soon forget how exactly they got there. Neither of these situations is conducive to successful learning. In order to succeed in these courses, you first need to learn how to read online textbooks and then how to complete online homework. Now, however, you should assess your current reading system by completing Activity 3.2.

Activity 3.2 Textbook Reading Assessment

This short assessment will help you understand your approach to reading. Many students don't read their textbook (hard copy or online) because they think it will not help them. This is far from the truth. Even students who do read the text may not do it effectively. Complete the self assessment to see where you stand.

1. Math instructors and students discuss when the best time is to read the textbook. Indicate which one is best for you and why?

When do you read your textbook?
_____ Before class
_____ After class
_____ Honestly, I don't read the textbook
Why?

2. When you read your textbook, do you use a system?
_____ Yes
_____ Sometimes
_____ No
How do you read the textbook?

3. Does reading your textbook help you improve math learning?
_____ Yes
_____A little
_____ No
_____ I don't read the textbook

4. If reading your textbook does not help you learn math, explain why you think this is true. Is there any way reading your text might help improve your math learning and grades? If reading the text does help you learn math, explain why in the same space below.

When to Read Your Textbook

Most students don't read math textbooks because in the past many math textbooks were poorly written. These books were difficult to understand, composed mostly of example problems, and written for instructors instead of students. Now, math textbooks are more student friendly and feature more support materials. When we discuss reading a math textbook, we are also focusing on the additional products that come with the textbook. This includes videos, online texts, problem hints, support websites and tutor sites.

Math instructors and students often debate over the best time to read a math textbook. Some instructors prefer that students read the textbook before coming to class. Other instructors prefer students read the textbook after class. If students read their textbook before going to class, they become familiar with key vocabulary words and concepts. You don't need to understand every bit of material when you read your book before class. Yet, understanding even just a third of the material will free up your mind to understand more material during a lecture.

For this reason, I recommend reading ahead two or three sections and putting question marks by material you don't understand. Make a list of the vocabulary words that will most likely appear in a lecture. When your instructor starts discussing the material, have your questions ready and take good notes. When they start discussing a topic you marked, pay special attention. If you do not understand your instructor's explanation, you MUST ask questions. If there is not enough time for questions, make an appointment with your instructor to go over the material. Reading the text before a lecture helps you better understand it and know when to ask questions.

Reading the textbook after a lecture also has its benefits. This method reinforces the material learned in class and further explains misunderstood information. Instructors who believe in this format think they can explain mathematical concepts better than the textbook or don't want you to get confused by its explanations.

Reading the textbook after a lecture helps students to remember notes taken during class. The textbook also explains mathematical concepts in different, more understandable ways. In addition, the textbook might cover material that was not discussed in the lecture that will help clarify a concept.

Reading a mathematics textbook before or after the lecture may depend on how well the book is written. It also depends on your learning preference. Try both ways and see which one works best.

10 Steps to Better Understand What You Read

Before practicing the Ten Steps to Understanding Reading Materials, you need to get to know your textbook. Each textbook has its own organizational pattern for presenting information. It is important to understand how the book works.

- Are there learning objectives at the beginning of the chapter that can be used as a checklist to make sure you are learning everything important?

- How are the vocabulary words highlighted? Are they just bold print? Are they in highlighted boxes?

- How are the mathematical rules highlighted?

- Does each section of the chapter have learning objectives?

- Are the homework problems at the end of the chapter arranged according to the chapter sections?

If you can't figure out how your textbook is organized, go to your instructor or a learning center to receive assistance in "figuring the book out." Once you understand how to use your book, then take the following steps and adapt them in a way that they work for you.

There are several appropriate steps in reading a math textbook:

Step One— *Skim the assigned reading material in order to get a general idea of what the chapter is about.* Skimming is an excellent skill to develop. First, it is an excellent way to get familiar with what will be covered in the next class. Second, as you sit down to study your math after the lecture, it helps you to see how all the "pieces of the puzzle" fit together. Third, after you have learned the material, it is a good strategy to use as a quick ten-minute review so that you do not forget what you learned.

Here are the steps I suggest:

- Read the chapter introduction and/or learning objectives and each section summary and/or learning objectives. As you read, try to see the connections between each section. Remember, when you skim, do not try to learn the material; you simply want to get an overview of the assignment.

- As you skim, think about similar math topics that you already know. What do you already know about the chapter objectives?

- As you skim the chapter, circle (using pencil) new words that you do not understand. You can also skim after learning the material, pretending you are a tutor explaining how each objective connects with one another. You can even explain in your own words what each vocabulary word means as if you were tutoring. This skimming also helps you remember what you have spent so much time learning.

Step Two — *While reading the textbook, highlight the material that is important to you.* However, do not highlight more than 50 percent of a page because the material is not being narrowed down enough for future study. If you are reading the textbook after the lecture, highlight the material that was discussed in the class. Material discussed both in the textbook and lecture usually appears on the test. The purpose for highlighting is to emphasize the important material for future study.

Step Three — *When you get to the examples, go through each step.* If the example skips any steps, make sure you write down each one of those skipped steps in the textbook for better understanding. Later on, when you go back and review, the steps are already filled in. You will understand how each step was completed. Also, by filling in the extra steps, you are starting to over-learn the material for better recall on future tests.

Step Four — *Revise your marks and highlights.* Maybe you marked them the first time while skimming. If you understand them now, erase the marks. If you do not understand the words or concepts, then reread the page or look them up in the glossary. Try not to read any further until you understand all the words and concepts.

Step Five — *Take notes from your math textbook on principles, properties and rules.* Taking meaningful notes after reading a math textbook helps students remember what they have read. These notes also serve as a review sheet for preparing for a test. This note-taking system is different from taking notes in the classroom. These notes become a quicker resource for information while completing

homework and are beneficial in learning math vocabulary. The steps are as follows:

- Before reading the math book, label the top of your notebook page with the chapter and section numbers. For example, at the top of the note page put Chapter 2.3 to 2.6.

- Divide the page into three columns. Label the left one "Terms," the middle one "Examples" and the third one "Definitions and Explanations."

- As you read about principles, properties or rules, write down their names, define them, give one or two examples and explain the process.

Terms	Example	Definitions/Explanation
Multiplication principle	$1/3x = -15$ $3(1/3x) = 3\,(-15)$ $x = -45$	Def. = for real numbers a, b, c, with c not = to 0, if a=b then ca=cb Multiply each side of the equation by 3 (this isolates the x). Multiply the other side by 3.

Step Six — *Learn math vocabulary words.* If you do not clearly understand some words, add these words to the note-taking glossary in the back of your notebook. Your glossary will contain the bold print words that you do not understand. You should have the book definition and the definition in your own words. If you have difficulty understanding the bold-print words, ask the instructor for a better explanation. You should know all the words and concepts in your notebook glossary before taking the test.

Step Seven — *If you do not understand the material, follow these eight points, one after the other, until you are comfortable with the information.*

1. Go back to the previous page and reread the information to maintain a train of thought. Make sure you have learned the previous information correctly.

2. Read ahead to the next page to discover

if any additional information better explains the misunderstood material.

3. Locate and review any diagrams, examples or rules that explain the misunderstood material.

4. Read the misunderstood paragraph(s) several times aloud to better understand its meaning.

5. Refer to your math notes for a better explanation of the misunderstood material.

6. Refer to another math textbook, computer software program or website that expands the explanation of the misunderstood material.

7. Define exactly what you do not understand and call your study buddy for help.

8. Contact your math tutor or math instructor for help in understanding the material.

Step Eight — *Reflect on what you have read.* Combine what you already know with the new information that you just read. Think about how this new information enhances your math knowledge. Prepare questions for your instructor on the confusing information. Ask those questions at the next class meeting.

Step Nine — *Review your math textbook notes and math glossary several times a week.* Anytime you have a spare five to ten minutes, review your notes or vocabulary words. These short periods of time allow you to study in little chunks and become confident in your understanding of the material. Try reviewing before the math lecture starts, between classes, or at lunch. Over a period of several weeks you will be amazed at how much you can learn. This process can ensure that you know the information before taking a test.

Step Ten — *Write anticipated test questions.* Research has noted that students have about 80 percent accuracy in predicting test questions. Think about what is the most important concept you just read and what

problems the instructor could give you that would test the knowledge of that concept. Make up four or five problems and add them to your problem log (this was part of your note-taking system). Indicate that these questions are from reading the textbook. Review the questions and answers before taking the next test. By using this reading technique, you have:

- Narrowed down the important material to be learned,

- Skimmed the textbook to get an overview of the assignment

- Carefully read the material and highlighted the important parts,

- Recorded important information into a three column note-taking system, and,

- Added to your note-taking glossary unknown words or concepts.

Now that you understand the benefits of reading your textbook, you need to decide when to read the text and how not to procrastinate. As mentioned earlier, it is best to read the text before doing your homework. Look at your study schedule and see when you have scheduled your homework time. Do you have time to read the textbook before that time, or do you want to include reading your textbook as part of your homework time?

When I ask students for the reasons they do not read the text, many tell me that they simply had other things to do. In almost every case, these other things were not that important. When we discuss this issue, students usually admit they do not like reading the text, and they use distractions as an excuse to get out of it. In most cases, these students claim that they have read their math texts in the past, and it did not help them learn how to complete problems. What these students don't realize, is that the only reason they experience ineffective study sessions is that they've never been taught how to correctly read a math text.

If you want to pass your math course, this is an absolutely vital skill. You cannot succeed without fully understanding your text.

How to Read an Online Textbook

Reading an online textbook differs a great deal from reading a traditional textbook. The objectives are the same—you still want to have a better understanding of math and eventually transfer information into your long-term memory—but because online texts come in many different formats, these books require much more preparation before reading.

Before reading an online text, you need to become familiar with how the e-book is formatted. Each online text or e-book has its own organizational pattern for presenting information and resources. It is important to understand how the book works. Before reading, you must ask yourself a series of questions.

- Are there learning objectives at the beginning of the chapter or chapter sections that can be used as a checklist?
- How are the vocabulary words highlighted? Are they bold print?
- Are they in highlighted boxes?
- Can you electronically highlight the text?
- Can you mark a page and come back to it?
- How are the mathematical rules highlighted?

- Does the chapter have a vocabulary check that can become your glossary?
- Does the chapter have highlights or review sections with definitions and concepts?
- Are there additional resources to support chapter readings?

If you have difficulty understanding how to use an online textbook, then go to your instructor, learning center or math lab to receive assistance. Understanding how to use the text improves your ability to learn math.

With that out of the way, it is time to get on to the specific steps you need to follow to read on online text. Note that these steps are similar to those given in the previous section for traditional textbooks. These steps, however, take into account the technological aspects that make reading an e-book unique.

The following 10 steps are designed to help you read and digest information from textbooks presented on computer screens, tablets, or other mobile devices.

Step One—*Click or swipe through the assigned reading material or section(s) pertaining to the homework.*

This is a good idea for many reasons. First, doing so gives you a general idea of the material covered in a given section and thereby gives you a leg up on your homework. Second, this gives you a good idea where to turn when you get stuck on a particular homework problem. Third, it makes it easier to review information before taking quizzes or tests.

To skim effectively, stick to the following pattern:

1. Read the chapter introduction or first page of the section.

2. In the chapter introduction, review the learning objectives. As you read, try to see the connections between each section.

3. As you skim the section(s), highlight new words you do not understand. If you are reading on a tablet, many applications allow you to drag your finger over a particular word or line.

Step Two — *Read with concentration.* Now it is time to highlight specific material within a text — not just vocabulary words, but key concepts and formulas. Remember, the purpose for highlighting is to emphasize the important material for future study and review. Click through the pages and use the electronic highlighting method to mark important material.

Step Three — *Take notes from your math chapter section.* For every example, review each step even if you know the steps. If the example skips any steps, mentally tell yourself the step. If you don't know the step ask for help. You will now understand how each step was completed. By mentally going through these steps you are preparing for your homework and are starting to over learn the material for better recall on tests.

Step Four — *Revise your marks and highlights.* Maybe you already marked them while skimming. If you understand them now, remove the highlight. If you do not understand the words or concepts, then reread the page or see if they are in the vocabulary check or chapter highlight.

Step Five — *Take notes from the text.* The notes should only be on the principles, properties, rules and concepts. Taking meaningful notes, either during or after reading the math textbook, helps students remember what they have read. These notes also serve as a review sheet while preparing for a test. This note-taking system is different from taking notes in the classroom.

The steps are as follows:

- Before reading your online math book, label the top of your notebook page with the chapter and section numbers. For example, at the top of the page write "Chapter 1.1 — 1.3."

- Divide the page into three columns. Label the left one "Terms," the middle one "Examples" and the third one "Definitions/Explanations."

- As you read, or after you read, write down the principles, properties rules or concepts that you do not know, writing the term, example and definition/explanation.

Step Six — *Develop a Math Glossary.* Review the math vocabulary from your notes, and if you do not clearly understand some words, add these words to the note-taking glossary in the back of your notebook. The back of your note-book should be labeled by chapter and section with a list of these vocabulary words.

Step Seven — *Develop a strategy for understanding difficult material.* If you did not understand the material, follow these suggestions to improve learning:

1. Click or swipe back to the previous page and reread the information to maintain a train of thought.

2. Click or swipe ahead to the next page to discover if additional information explains misunderstood material.

3. Locate and review any diagrams, examples or rules that explain the misunderstood material.

4. Read the misunderstood paragraph(s) several times aloud to better understand its meaning.

5. Replay any math videos pertaining to a confusing section.

6. Refer to another math textbook, YouTube videos, or other online resources.

7. Define exactly what you do not understand and contact your study buddy for help.

8. Contact your math tutor or math instructor for help in understanding the material.

Step Eight — *Reflect on what you have just read.* Combine what you already know with new information that you just read. Think about how this information enhances your math knowledge.

Step Nine — *Review your math notes and math glossary.* This review should occur every week. When you have a spare 10 minutes, review your notes or vocabulary.

Step Ten — *Write unticipated test questions.* Research has noted that students have about 80 percent accuracy in predicting test questions. Think about the most important concepts you just read and how those concepts could be turned into test questions.

How to Read a Single Online Chapter Section

Reading a section of an online text involves a condensed version of the steps listed above. In most cases you are reading this section of the chapter because you are having difficulty answering specific homework problems. With this in mind, the purpose of reading this section is mainly to answer the homework problems and prepare for quizzes or tests.

Step One — *Concentrate on important information as you read the section.* Click or swipe through the pages and use the electronic highlighter to mark the information relating to the problem. If you understand very little information, you should review the video and then reread the section.

Step Two — *Go through examples similar to your problem.* For those examples, review each step and compare those steps that are related to your problem. Write the problem steps next to your problem steps for comparison. Going through example problem steps helps you solve your problem.

Step Three — *Take notes from your math chapter section.* The notes should be related to the principles, properties, rules and concepts of the problem you don't understand. Take the notes the same way as mentioned in the previous section and expand the "Terms" section to include vocabualry words. These notes can be used to help you solve this problem or similar problems or review for quizzes or tests.

Step Four — *Find additional resources.* If you did not understand material, seek out YouTube videos or math-based websites that contain information specific to your problems.

Step Five — *Review your math notes.* This review should occur every week. Review your math notes before reading the next section or homework. This process will help you to become more successful in reading the sections and problem solving.

By using this technique you can:

- Better understand math book sections,
- Answer homework problems,
- Prepare for quizzes and tests,
- and recall information on your quiz or test day.

Activity 3.3 Textbook Reading Review

In the previous Textbook Reading Assignment, you indicated when you reviewed your textbook, how often you read the textbook, and how (or if) reading the textbook helped your learning. This activity involves revisiting these issues based on the new information you just learned. Reading your textbook with effective strategies (hardcopy or online) improves learning. The following self-assessment helps determine what you need to do to properly use these strategies. If you have already indicated that you do some of the following behaviors, just check them again to reinforce that behavior.

1. When are you going to read the textbook? Indicate which one is best for you and why?

_____ Before class
_____ After class

Why?

2. I will use the 10 Steps to for Reading a Textbook?

_____ Yes (for a hardcopy text)
_____ Yes (for an online text)

How are these strategies different from the strategies you have used before?

3. List three ways these reading strategies will improve your understanding of math.

    1

    2

    3

4. How are you going to take notes from your reading assignment, and when are you going to review the notes?

Chapter Three: Checklist for Knowledge and Behaviors

Put a check after understanding the knowledge statements and fill in the behavioral activities.

Chapter Knowledge

1. I understand that the major reason freshman give for making poor grades is lack of study time. ＿＿＿

2. I know that research says that most students lose 50% of the information learned in class by the next day. ＿＿＿

3. I know that research says that the subject studied last at night is best remember the next day.＿＿＿

4. I know that my biological clock will tell me the best time to study either morning, afternoon or night. ＿＿＿＿

5. I know that I need to focus on the number of hours a week to study math instead of daily study hours. ＿＿＿＿

6. I know that I need some social time during the week; however, too much social time can lead to poor grades. ＿＿＿＿＿

7. I know that reading the math text is more difficult than reading other texts. ＿＿＿＿＿

8. I understand that learning how to correctly read the math textbook will improve my learning and help me understand lecture material. ＿＿＿＿＿

9. I use "Ten Steps to Understanding Reading Material" as an excellent way to comprehend the math text. ＿＿＿＿＿

10. I understand that I need to read the single online chapter section before doing the problems. ＿＿＿＿＿

Behavioral Activities

1. I study math as soon as possible right after class. ＿＿＿＿

2. I have competed my Planning Use of Daily Time schedule. ＿＿＿＿＿

3. I am going to study math and do homework ＿＿＿＿＿ hours a week.

4. After taking the next math test, I will review my study hours to see if they need to be increased.＿＿＿

5. I have completed my Weekly Study Plan. ＿＿＿＿＿

6. I have chosen to make a(n) ＿＿＿＿＿ in my math class.

7. I reviewed my textbook to see how it is organized. ＿＿＿＿

8. I take notes when reading my math textbook. ＿＿＿＿

9. I developed strategies to help understand reading material when I get stuck. ＿＿＿

10. I developed a math glossary from my textbook.＿＿＿＿

Name: _____   Date: _____

Assignment for Chapter 3

Answer the following questions on a separate piece of paper.

1. How should your biological clock affect the times you schedule study time?

2. What are the reasons to monitor the number of hours a week you study math?

3. List two reasons for developing a study schedule.

4. Complete the Planning Use of Daily Time chart, select your math course grade, and select your overall GPA.

5. What should you do if you want to study 15 hours a week but only have 10 hours open on your schedule?

6. List three connections between math textbooks and homework.

7. When is the best time for you to read your math textbook?

8. Explain how taking notes while reading your textbook and developing a math glossary can improve math learning.

9. What are the reasons many students give for not reading the math textbook and how can this lower your grade?

10. List and describe the ten steps to reading a math textbook or an online math textbook.

How to Improve Your Homework Techniques

4

In Chapter 4
You will learn these concepts:

✓ How to effectively complete math homework

✓ How to use metacognitive techniques to solve problems

✓ How to effectively complete Web-based and online homework

✓ How to best use math labs and Learning Resource Centers

✓ How to work with tutors and classmates

Math Homework Techniques

Why do math instructors assign homework? That is a good question. I have asked this question to students, math instructors and math department chairs. Some of them knew the answer, but I was surprised when some of them, including the instructors, did not know the answer. Again, let me ask you the question, "Why do instructors assign math homework?"

Yes, you are correct. Homework is given not to waste time but to have you practice the math problems often enough to understand the mathematical concept that can be put into your abstract reasoning or long-term memory. In other words, you do math homework to remember how to do the problems during the test. However, just memorizing how to do the problems will create difficulty recalling how to do them on the test.

Math homework techniques help students at all levels. Doing your homework is an excellent time to practice problems as if on a test and to understand the mathematical concepts. Completing homework needs to be a learning experience.

Now that you know the reasons to do your homework, I have another question. "Has anyone taught you the best way to do your homework?" Probably not. The next section will answer that question.

Doing your homework can be frustrating or rewarding. Most students jump right into their homework, become frustrated and either stop studying or click on the help icon. These students usually go directly to the math problems and start working them without any preparation. When they get stuck on one problem, they flip to the back of the textbook for the answer. Then, they either try to work the problem backwards to understand the problem steps, or they just copy down the answer. Other students use Google or a phone application to automatically generate an answer. After getting stuck several times, these students will inevitably quit doing their homework assignment. Their homework becomes a frustrating experience, and they may even quit altogether.

Now that you know how some students do their homework, the next step is reviewing how you do your own homework.

To start the evaluation, complete Activity 4.1 (located on the next page).

Activity 4.1 Math Homework Assessment

This short self-assessment will help you understand how you approach your homework. Many students don't do all their homework because they believe doing every problem doesn't help them. Even students who do all the homework sometimes don't do it effectively.

1. Check the appropriate sentence that best describes your usual homework tactics.

    When doing homework:

    _____   I complete the entire assignment.

    _____   I finish some of the assignment.

    _____   Honestly, I don't really do my math homework.

    Does reading the math text help improve your math learning?

    _____   Yes

    _____   A little

    _____   Not at all

    _____   This question doesn't apply to me. I don't do my math homework.

2. If doing your math homework does not help you learn math, then explain why in the empty space below.

3. In the space below, explain how you typically approach doing your math homework:

10 Steps to Doing Your Math Homework

The following 10 steps are designed to help you complete traditional homework assignments from printed textbooks. If you are in an online class, go ahead and turn to the next section, "10 Steps to Doing Your Online or Computer-Based Learning Homework."

Step One — *Review the textbook material that relates to the homework.* You can also use your glossary and textbook notes in your notebook. A proper review will increase the chances of successfully completing your homework. If you get stuck on a problem, you will have a better chance of remembering the location of similar problems. If you do not review prior to doing your homework, you could get stuck and not know where to find help in the textbook.

Step Two — *Review your lecture notes that relate to your homework.* If you could not understand the explanation in the textbook on how to complete the homework assignment, then review your class notes.

Step Three — *Do your homework as neatly as possible.* Doing your homework — organized and neatly — has several benefits. When approaching your instructor about problems with your homework, he or she will

be able to understand your previous attempts to solve the problem. The instructor will easily locate the mistakes and show you how to correct the steps without having to decipher your handwriting. Another benefit is that, when you review for midterm or final exams, you can quickly relearn the homework material without having to decipher your own writing.

Example: Problem: 2 (a + 5) = 0. What property allows you to write the equation as 2a + 10 = 0? Answer: The distributive property.

Step Four — *Write down every step of every problem.* Even if you can do the step in your head, write it down anyway. This will increase the amount of homework time, but you are over-learning how to solve problems, which improves your memory. Doing every step is an easy way to memorize and understand the material. Another advantage is that when you rework the problems you did wrong, it is easy to review each step to find the mistake.

Step Five — *Understand the reasons for each step and check your answers.* Do not get into the bad habit of memorizing how to do problems without knowing the reasons for each step. Many students are smart enough to memorize procedures required to complete a set of homework problems. However, when slightly different problems are presented on a test, they cannot solve the problems. To avoid this dilemma, keep reminding yourself about the rules, laws, or properties used to solve problems. A good idea is to write each name of the rule, law or property by several of the homework problems. Then, the homework becomes a test review.

Example: Solve this equation:
$6x + 5 = 4x + 1$.

The answer is $x = -2$.

Now put this back into the equation:
$6(-2) + 5 = 4(-2) + 1$

Reduces to $-12 + 5 = -7$, which is $-7 = -7$.

If one side of the equation equals the other, you have the correct answer. If not rework the problem.

Once you know the correct reason for going from one step to another in solving a math problem, you can answer any problem requiring that property. Checking your homework answers should be a part of your homework process because it improves your learning and helps you prepare for tests. Check the answers of the problems for which you do not have the solutions. This may be the even-numbered or odd-numbered problems or the problems not answered in the solutions manual. You can also check your answers by substituting the answer back into the equation, doing the opposite function required to answer the question, or using one of the applications listed in Appendix A.

Step Six — *If you do not understand how to do a problem, refer to these points:*

1. Review the textbook material that relates to the problem.

2. Review the lecture notes that relate to the problem.

3. Review any similar problems, diagrams, examples or rules that explain the misunderstood material.

4. Refer to another math textbook, solutions guide, website, phone application, or online video to obtain a better understanding of the material.

5. Call a classmate.

6. Skip the problem and contact your tutor or math instructor as soon as possible for help.

Step Seven — *Always finish your homework by successfully completing problems.* Even if you get stuck, go back and successfully complete previous problems before quitting. You want to end your homework assignment with feelings of success.

Step Eight — *After finishing your homework assignment, recall to yourself or write down the most important learned concepts.* Recalling this information will increase your ability to learn these new concepts. This information can be placed in your textbook notes, glossary, or lecture notes, whichever you choose.

Step Nine — *Make up notecards or audio recordings containing hard-to-remember problems or concepts.* Notecards and audio recordings are excellent ways to review material for a test. More information on how to use these methods to improve learning is presented in Chapter Six.

Step Ten — *Getting behind in math homework is academic suicide.* As mentioned in Chapter One, math is a sequential learning process. If you get behind, it is difficult to catch up because each topic builds on the next. It would be like going to Spanish class without learning the last set of vocabulary words. The teacher would be talking to you using the new vocabulary, but you would not understand what was being said.

Do Not Fall Behind and Watch Out for Shortcuts!

To keep up with your homework, it is necessary to complete the homework every schoolday and even on weekends. Doing your homework one-half hour each day for two days in a row is better than one hour every other day. If you have to get behind in one of your courses, make sure it is not math. After using the 10 Steps to Doing Your Homework, you may be able to combine two steps into one. Find your best combination of homework steps and use them. Before moving on, take a breath. This study process seems very involved. However, if you adapt this process to work for you, this is what could happen:

- You will actually learn the math. This will help not only immediately but also in your future math courses.

- You will work with the math so much that it will land in your long-term memory, and you will not have to cram the night before the test.

- Imagine knowing how to do everything on the test the night before. Very little stress. A good night's sleep.

Watch Out for Shortcuts

When doing your math homework, you may get help from a friend or tutor. This friend or tutor wants to help you and should show you every step in working the problem. However, if you ever hear the statement "Let me show you a shortcut to solving this problem," BEWARE! Many students have told me that they were shown shortcuts to working problems and followed the steps. However, later on, they could not use the shortcuts to solve homework problems or test problems. Learning shortcuts can lead to over confidence and poorer grades. Some major problems with shortcuts are:

1. Shortcuts may require math knowledge above your math level.

2. Shortcuts may not be able to be used on similar problems.

3. Instructors may not want the shortcuts used on a test.

4. Shortcuts may not have a reference in the text to "fall back on."

5. Shortcuts are usually shown once and not remembered.

6. Shortcuts may be used by tutors or friends because they do not know how to work the problem step-by-step, and neither will you.

Not all shortcuts are bad, but you need to know the reasoning behind a shortcut. If a friend or tutor wants to show you a shortcut for solving a math problem, ask them for the rules or properties that support the shortcut. Once you understand the rule or property you can then apply the shortcut. Shortcuts are not bad when you understand the reasons behind them.

Using Metacognitive Techniques

Metacognition is a new concept that helps students improve their learning as they complete textbook and online homework. It mostly involves what students are thinking about when solving math problems. This is a self-monitoring process used to develop problem solving steps to find the solution to the problem. Memorization of problem steps instead of understanding the rules and principles to solve the problems leads to passive learning and unsuccessful problem solving. You need a model to follow when solving math problems.

The model of plan, monitor and evaluate is the framework for solving math problems. This model involves asking yourself questions when solving problems. Planning consists of understanding what the problem wants, the strategies to solve the problem, potential obstacles, understanding what information is required, doing the calculations and predicting the outcome. Monitoring is putting the steps in order, keeping one's place, identifying and finding errors, understanding when additional information is needed, knowing when to use another strategy and knowing when you have part of the answer. Evaluating includes knowing if the answer seems right (number sense), putting the answer back into the equation or doing the opposite of the function to see if the answer is correct and measuring the efficiency of the plan and monitoring.

Now that we know the theory about metacognition, let's apply it to solving some math problems. Let's look at the process for solving linear equations.

Solve: $-3(x-6) + 2 = 2(4x - 1)$

The first step is making a plan by asking yourself questions about solving linear equations. Some example questions to solve this equation are:

1. Question: What is a linear equation?

Answer: It must have at least one variable and some numerals or variables and an = sign but no exponents greater than one.

Example: $-3(x - 6) + 2 = 2(4x - 1)$

2. Question: Are there any ( ) ?

Answer: Yes. Then multiply the number or variable in front times everything inside the ( ).

Example: $-3(x-6)+2=2(4x-1)$
$-3x+18+2=8x-2$

3. Question: Are there like terms on the same side of the equation?

Answer: Yes. Then combine the like terms on the same side only.

Example: $-3x+18+2=8x-2$
$-3x+20=8x-2$

4. Question: Are there letters and/or numbers on both sides of the = ?

Answer: Yes. Then put the letters on one side and the numbers on the other side.

Example: $-3x+20=8x-2$
$-3x+20+2=8x-2+2$
$-3x+22=8x$
$3x-3x+22=8x+3x$
$22=11x$

5. Question: Is there a number attached to x?

Answer: Yes. Then divide both sides by the number that is attached to x.

Example: $\dfrac{22}{11}=\dfrac{11x}{11}$
$2=x$

6. Question: Does this seem to be the right answer?

Answer: Yes. The answer is about right. It is not too large.

7. Question: How can you find out if it is right?

Answer: Substitute the answer back into the equations and see if one side equals the other side.

Example: $-3(x-6)+2=2(4x-1)$
substitute 2 for x
$-3(2-6)+2=2(4(2)-1)$
$12+2=2(7)$
$14=14$

8. Question: Is this the right answer?

Answer: Yes. One side equals the other side.

The metacongnitive process involves planing, monitoring and evaluating. Step one is part of the plan, steps two through five involve a combination of planning and monitoring. Step six is the evaluation. Use this as a model of asking yourself questions while solving linear equations. Ask your instructor about exceptions to these problems. Now let's look at the steps for solving quadratic equations. What are some of the questions you need to ask yourself to solve $x^2 + 6x = 16$. The first step to planning is to ask yourself questions about quadratic equations. Some example questions to solve this equation are:

1. Question: What is a quadratic equation?

Answer: It has a square term and has an = sign.

Example: $x^2 + 6x = 16$

2. Question: Does one side of the equation equal to 0?

Answer: No. Then move the term from the right side to the left side by using the opposite sign.

Example: $x^2 + 6x = 16$
$x^2 + 6x - 16 = 16 - 16$
$x^2 + 6x - 16 = 0$

3. Question: Can you factor the left side of the equation

Answer: Yes.

Example: $(x + 8)(x - 2) = 0$

4. Question: Do we have two factors?

Answer: Yes.

5. Question: What are the factors?

Answer: $(x + 8)$ and $(x - 2)$

6. Question: Can you solve each equation?

Answer: Yes.

Example:
$$x + 8 = 0 \qquad x - 2 = 0$$
$$x + 8 - 8 = 0 - 8 \qquad x - 2 + 2 = 0 + 2$$
$$x = -8 \qquad x = 2$$

7. Question: You should have two solutions. Do you?

Answer: Yes. They are -8 and 2.

8. Question A: Does this seem to be the right answer?

Answer: Yes. They are two answers and they are not too large.

Question B: How can you find out if it is right?

Answer: Put the answers back.

Example:
$$x^2 + 6x = 16; \text{ Solution one is } x = -8$$
$$64 - 48 = 16$$
$$16 = 16$$

or

$$x^2 + 6x = 16; \text{ Solution two is } x = 2$$
$$4 + 12 = 16$$
$$16 = 16$$

Question C: Are these the right answers?

Answer: Yes. One side equals the other side.

Like the previous problem, step one is part of the plan, steps two and three are a combination of planning and monitoring, while step four is monitoring. Steps five and six are a combination of planning and monitoring. Step seven is monitoring again, while step eight is evaluating. This is a model you can use to help ask yourself questions while solving problems.

You can ask your instructor about exceptions to these problems. Using metacognition to solve math problems will increase your homework and test-taking success. You may ask yourself different questions based on the different types of problems.

These questions may come slowly at first, but they will speed up and become almost automatic, just like your basic multiplication tables. Your math instructors have already achieved this goal and can solve linear and quadratic equations almost at the speed of light. Don't be intimidated. It has taken them many years to accomplish these skills. With practice, some day you can be just as effective.

Metacognition in Class

Practice these metacognitive strategies in the classroom or when watching math support videos. When your instructor puts the problem on the board or you see it in a video, follow the model of plan, monitor and evaluate. Ask yourself questions such as:

- "Do I understand the problem?"
- "What is this problem asking me to do?"
- "How can I solve it using planning?"

The next step is to figure out the first step to the problem and see if the instructor writes down that first step. After doing this, move to the monitoring stage and start writing down the first step and anticipating the next steps.

As for the evaluation part of the process, pretend to check the instructor's steps to make sure they are done correctly (sometimes instructors do make mistakes). If you get confused with some of the steps, ask your instructor to clarify. By doing this, you are practicing metacognitive strategies in the classroom the same way you might while doing your homework.

Activity 4.2 Metacognitive Homework

Many students do not assess their thinking process for solving homework problems. This self-assessment will help you understand what you are thinking while working problems. This will allow you to use metacogntive strategies to solve similar problems.

1. Take one of your homework problems and write it down in the space below:

2. In the space below, write down what you are thinking as you solve the problem. In other words, describe your general approach to finding the correct answer:

3. Now write down a second similar homework problem and record what you are thinking while using the metacognitive model of plan, monitor and evaluate.

Homework problem:

Plan:

Model:

Evaluate:

Distance Learning, Computer-Based Learning, and Online Homework

Community colleges and universities are shifting more and more courses to the online and Computer-Based models. Both of these models require students to become self-learners and self-motivators. Computer-based classrooms require students to complete online homework without listening to lectures, and online courses require students to do just about everything on their own.

Many distance learning students have difficulty in communicating with their instructors and classmates. These students have told me that they do not know how or when to communicate with their instructor. Also, these students did not know that they could communicate with other students for support and help. As a result of this lack of communication, some of these students withdrew from their courses or made a lower grade than they'd intended.

Students in math classroom courses and distance learning math courses are having difficulty developing strategies for completing their required online homework assignments and learning the material. Students are used to doing homework with paper and pencil, not on the computer. Many of these students have told me that they completed the online homework and submitted it, only to realize later on that they have no homework to review for tests. Also, they had no homework to compare with other students or to use as a basis for in-class questions. In short, they did not know how to use online homework to improve their grades and learning. This is something that must be overcome.

These students need a system built specifically for doing online homework. This system needs to be just as detailed, perhaps even more so, than systems built for traditional, classroom-based math courses. With this in mind, over the next few sections, you'll learn:

- 10 Steps to Doing Your Homework (classroom and online).

- Where to find additional learning resources online.

- How to recall what you have learned

10 Steps to Doing Your Online Math Homework

In some courses, all or part of your homework may be assigned to be done online. This is usually the case if you are taking a distance-learning course, a hybrid or blended course, a Computer-Based Learning course, or a course where the computer is used as a part of the learning process. In addition, some lecture instructors may assign online homework as an alternative to homework done from the textbook. Whatever the case may be, you will need to develop study skills that can help you improve your online homework success and learning.

Doing your homework online can be a rewarding and enriching experience, but it can also be frustrating if you run into technical problems. Before you take a course that requires you to do homework online, you should ask yourself these questions:

1. Do I have easy access to computer equipment and software, including high-speed Internet access, to run the homework program?

2. Do I have the necessary computer skills to use the computer and software?

3. Am I comfortable doing my homework on the computer?

If you answered yes to all the questions, then you are ready to begin doing homework online! The 10 Steps to Doing Your Homework are still valid, but we will adapt the steps to online homework.

Step One — *Review the textbook material that relates to the homework.* This step is still essential when doing online homework. However, the software you are using may have an online textbook that has additional resources to help you learn concepts. Some programs provide you with lecture videos, animations, audio clips, and interactive exercises that you can practice working as you read through the examples in the multimedia textbook. Take advantage of these resources to help you learn the material.

Step Two — *Review your video lecture notes that relate to the homework.* If you are taking a course where your instructor does not lecture, you need to develop your own set of notes. Many software programs provide you with lecture videos. Watch these lectures and create your own notes as the presenter goes through the material. One big advantage of watching a video lecture is the ability to pause at crucial points and watch a segment over again if you need further review. In a live lecture, this is obviously not possible, and some students find it difficult to take good notes when the instructor moves too fast.

Step Three — *Do your homework as neatly as possible.* Although you will be doing your homework online, it remains important to do your work on paper and keep it in a notebook. Then, if you have a question about the homework, or if you disagree with the answer given by the program, you will be able to refer to your notes when discussing the homework with your instructor.

Step Four — *When doing your homework, write down every step of the problem.* First, write down the problem statement. This is especially important when doing online homework since many programs generate different problems for each student.

If you do not write down the problem, it can be difficult for you or your instructor to figure out what the original problem was. Next, solve the problem and show each and every step. Finally, enter the answer into the program. It is essential that you enter the answer in the correct wording and format. For example, if the program asks you to enter the answer as a fraction, and you enter the answer as a decimal, your answer may be marked wrong.

Step Five — *Understand the reasons for each problem step and check your answers.* Software programs check your answers and give you immediate feedback. This is one of the major advantages of doing homework online. If you get an answer incorrect, use the feedback along with your notes to try and figure out where you made the mistake. The program may also give you another opportunity to work the problem, perhaps with different numbers, and you should take advantage of this option. These programs also reinforce you for trying the problems by giving you positive statements when you get them correct. This makes many students feel good. However, you are not given positive statements for reading the text or watching a video. You can reinforce yourself for completing these tasks by learning more math and making better grades.

Step Six — *If you do not understand how to work the problem, use the resources provided by the software to learn how to do the problem correctly.* For example, you can ask the

program to guide you through the solution one step at a time. Use this approach to learn how to solve the problem. You may also be able to view an example that is similar to the problem you are trying to solve. You may also want to review the video lectures, multimedia textbook, or other online resources to help you understand the concepts.

Step Seven — *Always finish your homework by successfully completing problems.* With online homework, it's easier to end your homework session with feelings of success, since you can usually redo problems until you get the correct solution. Many students find that online homework not only helps them understand the concepts more readily, but it also gives them a boost in morale because of the immediate and positive feedback.

Step Eight — *After finishing your homework assignment, recall to yourself or write down the most important learned concepts.* This is still an important step when doing online homework, so resist the temptation to skip this step.

Step Nine — *Make up notecards containing hard-to-remember problems or concepts.* Some programs will provide students with ready-made notecards, and you can print these out and use them as starting points for your own notecards.

Step Ten — *Stay on schedule.* In a distance-learning, hybrid, or computer-aided course, there may not be fixed deadlines for each homework assignment, and students may be allowed to work at a flexible pace. However, if the course must be completed by the end of the term, it is better to pace yourself and complete the work in a timely manner rather than rushing to complete the bulk of the work just before the end of the term. Be sure to complete the online homework assignments in order. Math is still a sequential learning process regardless of how you do your homework!

Activity 4.3   Establishing Study Period Goals

Before beginning your homework, it is important to establish goals for the study period. Do not just grab a coke and chips, sit down and turn to the homework problems (whether in a textbook or in a computer program). Ask yourself this question, "What am I going to do tonight to become more successful in math?" By setting up short-term homework goals and reaching them, you will feel more confident about math. This will greatly improve your motivation to succeed.

Study-period goals are set up either on a time-line basis or an item-line basis. Studying on a time-line basis is studying math for a certain amount of time. Studying by item-line basis means you will study your math until you have completed a certain number of homework problems.

No matter what homework system you use, remember this important rule: Always finish a homework session by understanding a concept or doing a homework problem correctly. Do not end a homework session with a problem you cannot complete. You will lose confidence by thinking about the last problem you didn't complete or understand instead of all the ones you did understand. If you did quit on a problem you could not solve, return and rework problems you have done correctly.

Before your next homework assignment, set up your study period and homework goals by using "I" statements. For example, "I will do homework for an hour, then take a break." Or, "I will record vocabulary words in my glossary."

Goal 1:

Goal 2:

Goal 3:

Goal 4:

How to Use Math Labs, Learning Resource Centers and Distance Learning Resources

Learning how to use your Math Lab, Tutoring Center, or Learning Resource Center (LRC) can improve your grades. This is also true of those students who learn to thrive in computer-based classrooms, which require mandatory attendance. What follows is a reminder of already discussed resources.

Many students are unaware of the tutorial and learning resources offered at their institutions. Some find out about these resources after they are failing, which in most cases is too late. You need to find the location of learning resources and how to utilize them as soon as possible after course registration.

Some colleges and universities have math labs, LRCs, Academic Enrichment Centers, computer labs, Student Support Services, Veteran Services, Disabled Student Services or other specialized labs to help students. Math Labs and LRCs may also have a list of private tutors. You should ask your instructor or counselor where to get help in math. Do not forget to ask fellow students for recommendations. In the meantime, here are a few resources available at most math labs.

Computer Programs

Locate the computer program that best goes with your text. It may be the computer software offered by the textbook publisher or commercially bought software. Ask if you can copy it and use it at another location or on your own computer. Review the other available software programs to find the one that fits your needs. Ask the staff what they recommend. Newer computer programs are more user friendly.

Web-Based Programs

Most book companies have Web-supported materials to support student learning. These support areas could be an online tutor service, call-in tutor service, or extra homework problems and their solutions. Ask your instructor or lab supervisor about these support materials. If your text does not have these support materials, go to the Web and find them yourself. For a few examples of useful homework applications, see Appendix A.

Apps

When you cannot make it to the tutor lab or math lab, consider trying one of countless phone or tablet applications available for Apple and Android devices. Developers have created hundreds of applications for learning and practicing key math concepts. These applications are no replacement for face-to-face interaction, but they are useful nonetheless.

Tutoring

Most students believe that tutoring is the best learning resource. However, research has shown that the sessions are useless if the tutor is untrained. Try to work with a trained tutor who has had your course. Explain to the tutor your learning preference and suggest that he or she tutor you based on this preference.

Example 1: If you are an auditory learner, then have the tutor orally explain to you how to solve the problem. Then repeat back what the tutor said (in your own words). Use a recorder or phone-app to record the tutor's explanation so you can play it while doing your homework. Make sure the tutor does not just work the problem for you without explaining the reasons for each step.

Example 2: If you are a visual learner, have the tutors write down the steps to solve the problem. Also, write down the reasons for each step or reference text pages for the reasons. If the tutor cannot write it down for you, write down the steps yourself and ask the tutor to review the steps.

Try not to schedule your tutoring sessions around lunch time since it is usually the busiest time of the day. Have your questions ready from your previous homework assignments. Focus on the concepts you do not understand, not just on how to work the problem. The more specific you are about your homework problems, the more tutorial

help you will receive. Do not expect miracles! If you tell your tutor, "I have a test in twenty minutes and do not understand anything about chapter six!" — about all the tutor can do is offer to pray for you. However, past experiences have shown that those who have previously helped themselves to tutoring are most likely to be rewarded with good grades.

Practice Tests

Use practice tests to find out what you do not know before the real test. Ask if the math lab/LRC offers practice tests. Take these practice tests at least two days before the real test. This will give you at least one day to find out how to work the missed problems and another to review for the test. The more realistic practice tests you take, the better you will do on the real test. Make sure practice tests are timed and do not use any of your notes or the text.

Assessment Instruments

Assessment instruments can be used to place you into the correct course, locate your math weakness and help you understand your learning strengths and weaknesses. If you are not sure that you have been placed into the correct course, ask to take a placement test. Being placed into the correct course is a must to pass math. Ask if the lab has diagnostic math tests to locate your weaknesses. Ask about other assessment instruments, which can be used to help improve your learning.

Other helpful items include, manipulatives, models, posters, graphing calculators, YouTube videos and Google searches.

Manipulatives

If a picture is worth a thousand words, then a model is worth a million for the kinesthetic/tactile learner. If you are one of these learners, ask for what may be called "manipulatives" or "3-D models." Manipulatives and models are concrete representations of a concept that you can physically touch. A good example of a manipulative is the Hands On Equation. The

Hands on Equation uses a simulated balance beam with top like objects to represent variables and dice to represent numbers. Your math lab can order the Hands On Equations by going to www.Borenson.com. Some students have made their own manipulative by using magnetic plastic numbers and letters that are put on a metal board from child games.

Students also go to sign shops and purchase the numbers and letters. The students then set up an equation by using the manipulative and moving the numbers and letters around to solve it.

Students also use the letters to represent rules such as the distributive property. You can also use these manipulatives to understand more difficult mathematical problems.

The calculator is another excellent learning tool for students beginning in pre-algebra and developmental algebra. Graphing calculators match the dynamic cognitive and the kinesthetic/tactile (hands on) learning styles.

Examples: On the board put down $a(b + c) =$. Then on the other side of the equation take additional letters and place them to represent $ab + ac$. Now you have $a(b + c) = ab + bc$. Now do the steps over again until your learn it. Then put numbers in to represent the letters. Such as $2(3 + 4) = (2)(3) + (2)(4)$. Now do the multiplication on each side of the equation and you will get $14 = 14$.

Use the graphing calculator to see what happens when you add numbers to the equation. You can see the graph move and then understand the effects. This is an excellent way for trial-and-error learners (dynamic) to understand the equations. If you are in high-level courses, ask for connections intended for uploading graphing calculator programs from a computer. It is important to remember, however, some colleges/universities would rather you learn developmental math without using a calculator. For this reason, you should always speak with your professors and counselors before relying on any technological help.

In general, learning math is a lot like learning to ride a bicycle. You can watch someone else do it, but you only learn by trying it yourself. You must believe in yourself and keep at it. Even if you start off wobbly, as long as you keep peddling, you are riding. But if you do not believe in yourself enough to keep peddling, you will fall. In time, you will take off the training wheels and wonder why you ever needed them. Even if you get rusty after a long absence, you will never again need training wheels.

Math is also something you learn by trying it yourself. Others can assist you with techniques, but in order to make it stick, you need to learn math on your own. As long as you keep trying, you are learning to think mathematically, and you will be able to do it. In the future, even after a long time away from math, you will remember that you were able to master math before and with a little review you still can.

To find other math manipulatives online, click on the "Student Resources" section on AcademicSuccess.com. The website lists numerous helpful resources, many of which are free.

Distance Learning Resources

For many students, additional outside resources are a necessity for doing well in a course. These outside resources supplement online instruction and in some cases may become primary instruction. The learning resources be either traditional or non-traditional. Traditional learning resources include textbooks, private tutoring, tutor centers, adult education centers, libraries, study skills training, YouTube, online videos, and commercial computer programs. Non-traditional resources include call-in tutor centers, online tutor centers, commercial online tutor centers, websites, applications, or Google. These resources often enhance your learning.

Learning resources can also be categorized based on location. There are campus-based, community-based and personal resources. Campus-based resources are becoming very important because of the unexpected number of students who take both distance-learning courses and regular classroom courses. Students who are distance learners and cannot visit the campus look for local community resources to support their learning. Personal resources, such as tablets, have tremendously expanded because of the need to support distance-learning students. Taking advantage of these resources, especially early in the term, can increase your learning and grades. Try to find out what academic resources are available before enrolling in a distance-learning course in math. It doesn't have to be just you and the course. You can always get additional help.

Distance-learning students who have access to campus resources may want to go to the college or university website. This website should give you resource information needed for further contacts. You may want to contact the math lab, learning center, assessment center, library, returning adult center or any other place that can assist in you. You want to ask them the following questions:

1. Is tutoring by appointment or is it drop-in?
2. When is the best time to get tutoring?
3. Do you have evening hours for tutoring?
4. Do you have computer programs to assess my study skills and learning?
5. Do you have any computer programs to assess study skills and learning styles?
6. Can resource books be checked out?
7. Do you have a homework hotline?
8. What other learning resources do you have?
9. Do you have any locations that have these resources in my area?

Asking these questions will give you a good idea of the additional support that you can use on your campus. If it is too far to visit the campus to obtain this, look in your community to see if there are resources. Some of the places you can look are:

1. The local community, junior or technical college.
2. The adult high school center
3. Goodwill learning centers
4. County libraries
5. Commercial tutor centers such as Sylvan Learning Center or Hunting Learning Center
6. Private tutoring

Once a resource is located, you can ask them some of the same questions that you would ask the on-campus resources. Personal resources are accessible from your home and can supplement your learning.

Personal resources have greatly expanded over the last several years to include all sorts of help aids and materials. Some of the personal resources include:

1. Private in home tutoring
2. Educational TV
3. Live telephone tutoring
4. Online book ordering
5. YouTube videos
6. Online mini-lessons, algebra models, and worksheets
7. Online automated algebra problem solving
8. Zoom tutoring
9. Skype tutoring
10. FaceTime tutoring

Tutoring with trained tutors can be a great benefit to your learning. Some of these tutors will come to your home. You can find tutors online or get references by calling high school and college math departments or by asking your online instructor.

Make sure that the tutors are trained or they have references that you can call. Tutors can be a great help in improving your learning, but most students wait too long to use them. As soon as you are in trouble, or if you anticipate the need for assistance, find it immediately. Don't wait until you are failing.

Internet Resources

Online mini-lessons, algebra models, worksheets, virtual algebra solutions, and sites that solve math problems are on certain websites. Some websites are free. Others require a registration fee. Some of these sites have advertisements that pay for the site. You might want to review the sites under Student Math Practice and Learning Sites at AcademicSuccess.com—Student Resources. The sites are arranged by math course name with supplemental learning in calculator skills, virtual flash cards and video lessons.

Using these online sources can improve your math learning and skills. Distance learning students can also find free sites that will solve their submitted math problems.

Additional learning resources can make the difference in being successful in a distance-learning course. Explore the different resources to see which ones meet your preference style and time constraints. If you are not sure which learning resource meets your needs, then try several of the different learning resources to discover which one best improves your learning.

See Appendix A for additional sources.

Using Google and YouTube to Solve Problems

Another way to use the Internet to solve homework problems is to Google the type of homework problem or to look for that type of problem on YouTube.

To Google the problem, you need to define the type of problem. Do this by turning to the textbook or homework section you are working on and looking for the heading. For example, if the section is titled "Dividing a Polynomial by a Monomial," enter the phrase exactly in the search bar. Doing this usually brings up numerous helpful websites. You

may have to click on serveral before you find the best resource for your particular learning preference, so do not focus on the first link you find unless it is immediately useful.

YouTube is also a great option. The website features thousands of math videos, which usually show the step-by-step processes required to solve specific types of math problems. For many visual and auditory learners, this is the best way to learn. Watching an expert solve a problem and listening to him or her describe the steps allows these students to grasp concepts much more quickly. If you are one of these students, don't hesitate to facilitate your reading sessions with any of the resources described above.

Once you discover which resources or videos work best for you, make sure to save them to your bookmarks. This will make it extremely easy to return to them in the future. This way, these Internet resources will become a part of your textbook reading process.

Make a Resource Plan

Now that you've learned about the different resources, it's time to make a plan on which resources you'll use to help you improve your learning. You need to have a discussion with LRC staff to see which resource are best for your math class. They know the answers based on items that are checked out or used. They may even have workshops on different topics that improve learning. For example, instructors may have given the LRC the URLs to their course's YouTube videos.

If you are in a distance learning class, make sure to ask the instructor which resources are recommend. In addition, many distance learning classes set up chatrooms so you can communicate with other students. you may suggest a Skype session with some of the students to form a study group. There are many distance learning resources to choose.

Make a plan to try several resources and decide which ones are best for you.

Activity 4.4 Establishing Math Lab, LRC, Tutoring Center, and Distance Learning Resources

Many students are unfamiliar with the math lab, LRC, and distance learning resources provided by their colleges. Students must locate and learn how to use additional resources to improve grades. Complete the survey and resource lists printed below, then summarize the resources you have used or will use.

1. In the space below, list the location(s) and hours of your college's math lab or LRC (there may be more than one).

2. List the tutor times and names that match your course and schedule.

3. List the times and locations for any ongoing group learning sessions. This includes Supplemental Instruction, Peer Assistance Learning, and group study sessions for your course.

4. List the location and times for any support workshops on subjects such as test anxiety, test-taking, test review and final exam review.

5. List and describe three apps you have used or will use to improve your learning.

6. List and describe two distance learning resources you can use for any course. Summarize your resources:

How to Work Effectively with Tutors and Classmates

Redesigned math courses require more independent learning outside the classroom. This means students now need to begin tutoring the first week of class to review forgotten or unlearned prerequisite math skills. Different students react to this tutoring in different ways. Some claim tutoring only further confuses them. Others indicate that they could not pass without it. What explains this disparity? Some students have learned how to become a better tutoree than others. Effective tutoring requires preparation before sessions and continues as a team approach, which requires student and tutor effort. Take the following steps, and you should be OK:

1. The best time for tutoring is right after class.

2. Schedule tutoring at least three times a week and put it in your phone's calendar.

3. Ask for permission to take pictures of difficult problems.

4. Ask for permission to record explanations of difficult problems.

5. Take effective notes, leaving blank lines between problem steps you don't understand.

6. During tutoring and after, understand that the person holding the pencil is the one doing the learning.

7. Show tutors your notes so that they can see how the instructor solves problems.

8. Tell your tutor your learning preference.

9. Suggest that the tutor teach you in your preferred learning preference.

10. Visual learners need color coded numbers and variables to aid memory.

11. Show the tutor pictures of difficult problems from class.

12. Take pictures of tutored problem steps for review.

13. Auditory learners should play back recorded explanations of difficult problems.

14. Auditory learners should also ask the tutor to explain how to work problems.

15. Use "talk out loud" strategies to tell your tutor exactly what you are thinking.

16. Have your tutor show you how to use math Apps to improve learning.

17. Once you find tutors that match your learning preference, stay with them.

18. Finish tutoring sessions with problems you can complete.

Students also use Zoom for tutoring. In this case, they can use similar strategies by holding documents up to the camera and recording sessions. All learners can use these multimodality learning strategies. Start off by implementing a few and continue to other strategies to discover which ones are best for you.

Communicating with Your Classmates

Communicating with your classmates can be a challenge and a benefit. Many distance-learning courses have group chatrooms. These chatrooms are live or the messages can be posted. The instant message capability of many email systems can set the stage for study groups. In the classroom, you also need other students' email addresses so you can keep up with assignments and help each other with difficult problems.

You need to have a classmate you can count on in case you miss class or have questions when doing your homework. Group learners can especially benefit from classmates who are taking the same course. You can also strike up working relationships with students in the math lab. If possible, find a classmate who knows more about math than you do. Ask your instructor which students would work well with you. Meet this classmate several times a week to work on problems and to discuss math. If you miss class, get notes from this person, so you will not fall behind. Then build a study group for learning and support.

It is also smart to call this classmate when you get stuck on homework. This way you can solve problems over the phone, Skype, or Facetime. Do not sit for half an hour trying to work one problem. This will destroy your confidence, waste valuable time, and possibly damage your relationship with your classmate. Think how much you could have learned by trying the problem for 15 minutes and then calling a classmate for help. Spend, at the maximum, 15 minutes on one problem before going on to the next problem or calling your classmate. Remember that you are part of a team.

As with any online endeavor, it is important to remember that everything you write, whether on a message board or on Facebook is permanent. If you post something on a social media platform, you must assume your professor will wind up seeing it. This means that you should NEVER post anything negative about your instructor nor complain about a bad test score. I have seen students who tweet something about a classmate or a teacher wind up getting in trouble for what they thought were harmless comments. When writing about school-related matters, always make sure to use appropriate language.

Communicating Through Online Applications

Thanks to programs such as Skype, Facetime, and Zoom, it is now possible for students to conduct face-to-face study sessions from anywhere in the world. These programs are particularly useful for online students and groups of classmates who want better access to their peers outside of class.

When setting up a video-based study session, come just as prepared as you would for a traditional meeting. Make sure to have your textbook, notes, and other materials within reach. This is not a phone situation. Your classmate can see you and everything you are doing. They will know if you are ill-prepared, so if you want a continued collegiate relationship with these people, it is important to treat the situation with respect.

Example: If you are using a laptop to join an online study session, do not look down at your phone to check your social media feeds. Stay focused on what your classmates say, and engage with the conversation. This way, you will earn your classmates' respect.

Another important feature of these applications is how they allow you to share the contents of your computer screen. While this feature works differently in each program, all major video-call services allow you to show your classmate your notes, PowerPoint slides, and other materials. Before conducting an online study session, make sure you know how these features work. This will save you time, as you won't have to hold your notes up to the screen. In many cases, you won't even have to read them aloud.

Activity 4.5 Establishing Tutoring Resources, and Working with Your Classmates

Many students have difficulty learning math in their campus-based and online courses. Luckily, tutoring and technology has helped improve learning and emotional support. In the previous section, you reported basic tutor information. Now you need to develop more effective tutoring strategies, as well as plan on how to better learn from your classmates. Complete the questions below to develop more effective strategies.

1. Effective tutoring requires preparation before tutoring sessions. To improve learning, list and describe three strategies you can use before you visit your tutor.

2. Effective tutoring also requires effective strategies *during* tutor sessions. List and describe three visual learning strategies you can use.

3. Additionally, tutoring requires auditory strategies to improve learning. List and describe three auditory strategies you can use during tutoring sessions.

4. Classmates can also help you with your learning. List the names of three classmates whom you can contact for help.

5. List two ways you plan to meet your classmate(s) in person, as well as the benefits of doing this.

6. List and describe two online strategies you can talk to classmates about to help you solve math problems, as well as the benefits of doing this.

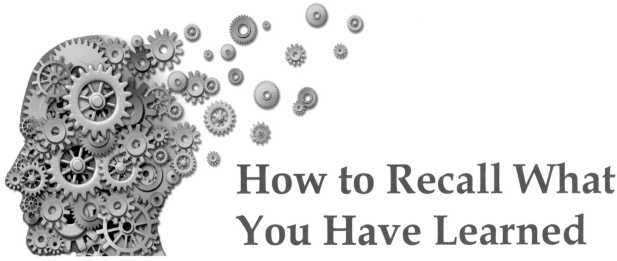

How to Recall What You Have Learned

After completing your homework problems, a good visual learning technique is to make notecards. Notecards are 3x5 index cards on which you place information that is difficult to learn or material you think will be on the test.

On the front of the notecard, write a math problem or information that you need to know. Color code important information in red or blue. On the back of the notecard, write how to work the problem or give an explanation of important information. Make notecards on important information you might forget. Every time you have five spare minutes, pull out your notecards and review them. Glance at the front of the card, repeat to yourself the answer and check yourself with the back of the card. If you are correct and know the information on a card, do not put it back in the deck. Mix up the cards you do not know and pick another card to test yourself. Keep doing this until there are no cards left that you do not know.

If you are an auditory learner, use a digital recorder or phone application just like the notecards. Record important information like you would on the front of a notecard, then leave a blank space on the recording. Record the answer. Play the audio file back. When you hear the silence, pause the recording, then say the answer out loud to yourself. Un-pause the recording and see if you were correct. You can use this technique in the car while driving to college or work.

Review What You Have Learned

After finishing your homework, close the textbook and try to remember what you have learned. Ask yourself these questions, "What major concepts did I learn tonight?" or "What test questions might the instructor ask on this material?"

Recall for about three to four minutes the major points of the assignment, especially the areas you had difficulty understanding. Write down questions for the instructor or tutor. Since most forgetting occurs right after learning the material, this short review will help you retain the new material.

Another great time to review your notes is right after completing a homework assignment. Make sure you know what section you finish to keep track of your progress. Look at the key words and repeat them to yourself or write them down on flash cards. Review the flash cards as often as you can, and write down any websites that you find helpful, including links to YouTube videos.

For online homework, open up these sites on your computer for a second review, then bookmark them so you can use them in the future. This is an especially good strategy if you do not have a math textbook or your textbook is online. In this scenario, your online bookmarks work the same way a real bookmark would in a tradtional text.

Chapter Four: Checklist for Knowledge and Behaviors

Put a check after understanding the knowledge statements and fill in the behavioral activities.

Chapter Knowledge

1. I understand the reasons instructors assign homework. _____

2. I understand that without a homework system students can become frustrated when doing their homework. _____

3. I know that it is important to follow the 10 Steps to Doing Your Math Homework until I become comfortable using them as part of my study routine. Then I can adjust the ten steps to make my own efficient system. _____

4. I understand that getting behind in math homework is a major problem and leads to failure. _____

5. I understand that I need to take time after completing my homework to recall what I have learned. This will help me retain new information in long-term and abstract reasoning. _____

6. I know that the metacognitive model for homework has three steps: plan, monitor and evaluate. _____

7. I know that applying the 10 Steps for Doing Online Homework to distance learning courses (or required online homework) can increase my math learning. _____

8. I understand that learning how to use math lab/LRC resources that match my learning preference can enhance learning. _____

9. I know to use practice tests at least two days before a test. This way, I will figure out what I don't know *before* rather than *during* the test. _____

10. I understand that distance learning courses are usually more difficult than classroom courses and require more time management. _____

Behavioral Activities

1. I read the related textbook section or reviewed my notes before starting my homework. _____

2. I immediately work several homework problems after class to make sure I understand necessary skills. _____

3. I work all assigned homework problems by the due date. _____

4. I use Metacognitive homework techniques to solve problems. _____

5. On difficult problems, I develop a series of questions to ask myself. _____

6. I review material to help keep it in my long-term memory. _____

7. I have selected three learning resources to help with my classroom or distance learning courses. _____

8. I have selected five tutor strategies to make me a better participant _____.

Name: _____   Date: _____

Assignment for Chapter 4

Answer the following questions on a separate piece of paper.

1. Why is it important to complete your math homework?

2. What should you do before starting your math homework?

3. What are the reasons for writing down every problem step while doing your homework?

4. List and describe the 10 Steps for Doing Your Math Homework or Online Homework.

5. Describe how you can use metacognitive strategies in the classroom or online course.

6. What are your best math lab or Learning Resource Center resources?

7. List and describe how you use three of the apps in Appendix A to improve your tutor sessions and math lab learning.

8. List and describe five resources you can use to improve online or classroom learning.

9. List and describe three strategies to help you recall what you have learned.

10. List the ways you are electronically communicating with your classmates on solving difficult problems.

Managing Anxiety and Taking Math Tests

5

In Chapter 5
You will learn these concepts:

✓ The causes of math anxiety and test anxiety

✓ The effects of test anxiety on learning

✓ How to reduce test anxiety

✓ Why attending class is not enough to pass tests

✓ Ten steps to better test taking

✓ How to analyze test errors for improvement

Understanding Math Anxiety

Math anxiety is a relatively new concept in education. During the 1970s, certain educators began using the terms "mathophobia" and "mathemaphobia" as a possible cause for a child's unwillingness to learn math. Modern psychologists define math anxiety as an extreme emotional and/or physical reaction to a negative attitude toward math.

Math anxiety affects students in many different ways. It sometimes manifests as tension, which interferes with the manipulation of numbers and the solving of math problems during tests (Richardson and Suinn, 1973). It also includes the panic, helplessness, paralysis and mental disorganization that occurs in some students when they are solving math problems. This discomfort varies in intensity and results from previous experiences in past learning situations (Tobias, 1978). There is a strong relationship between low math confidence and high math test anxiety.

Math anxiety is common among college students. Counselors at a major university recently reported that one-third of students enrolled in behavior therapy programs—usually offered through counseling centers—have problems with math anxiety. It has been shown that math anxiety exists among many students who do not suffer from other tensions. It frequently occurs in students with a poor high school math background. Roughly half of students enrolled in developmental math courses suffer from some form of math anxiety. Though students in high-level courses occasionally show symptoms as well, symptoms are usually worse for developmental students. Today, math anxiety contributes to the reduction of STEM majors around the world, as it often results in failure (Foley, et.al, 2017). It is real, but it *can* be overcome.

Math anxiety is divided into three separate anxieties: Math Test Anxiety, Numerical Anxiety and Abstraction Anxiety. Math Test Anxiety involves the anticipation, completion and feedback of math tests.

Numerical Anxiety refers to everyday situations that involve numbers and arithmetic calculations. Numerical anxiety affects students who are trying to figure out the proper amount for a tip, thinking about mathematics, doing math homework or listening to a math lecture.

Abstraction Anxiety involves working with variables and mathematical concepts used to solve equations. Some students experience all three types of math anxiety; others deal with only one.

Most of the students I have worked with deal with Math Test Anxiety and Abstraction Anxiety. These students do not have any anxiety with numbers, but often struggle with algebra and other symbol-heavy math. Unfortunately, these symbols are extremely common in college math courses.

Causes of Math Anxiety

Since math anxiety is a learned condition, its causes are unique to each student. Nevertheless, math anxiety is almost always rooted in an individual's past experiences. Bad experiences in elementary school are one of the most common sources for students' math anxiety: coming in last in math races at the blackboard, watching a classmate finish a problem twice as fast as they do, or teachers saying, "That's okay. You just aren't good in math; you are better in English." When asked, many students with math anxiety indicate that they were made fun of when trying to solve math problems at the chalkboard. This is by far the most common story I hear when working with students. Heckled students have a hard time letting go of painful memories. Harsh words and experiences remain with these students; when they walk into a classroom or open a math book, these bad experiences often play back in their minds.

A 56-year-old student once indicated to me that he had a great deal of fear that his instructor might call him to the board. Even if he knew how to do a problem, he was terrified at the thought of having to display that knowledge to his peers.

Example: Over the years, math anxiety is reinforced and even increases in magnitude. In fact, many math anxious students — now 30, 40 and 50 years old — still have extreme fear about working math problems on the board. These bad memories linger well into adulthood.

Being embarrassed by family members also causes math anxiety. According to a recent study, many students claim that their parents routinely try to help them with math and this sometimes leads to serious trauma. These students say that tutoring from their guardians, mainly their fathers, often results in scolding when they are not able to complete problems. One student reported that his father hit him every time he got a multiplication problem wrong.

Brothers and sisters also tease one another about being dumb in math. This is particularly true of boys telling girls that they cannot do math. When people hear these statements enough times, they often start to believe them and associate these bad feelings with math. For some students, just hearing the word "math" triggers a response of anxiety as they consciously or unconsciously recall bad feelings or memories.

A good example of this is a student who I worked with who had completed her BS degree 15 years ago at a college that did not require much math. She was returning to college to be an elementary school teacher, which required her to take math and a placement test. As soon as I mentioned that she had to take math, she said, "I can't do math, and I will have to wait a few days to get psychologically ready to take the math placement test." She indicated her old anxiety feelings rushed through her, and she almost had an anxiety attack. This is an extreme but true example of math anxiety. In most cases math anxiety is not this bad, but remains disruptive enough to cause learning and testing problems.

Those who don't have math anxiety still have to understand it. This way they can help their classmates who need support. Also, if you do not have math anxiety now, you may develop it in the future. One way to overcome math anxiety is to find out when it first occurred and how it is still affecting you. A math autobiography is an excellent way to review previous math experiences and to learn how to overcome math anxiety. To find out more about writing a math autobiography, complete the first two activities in this chapter.

How Math Anxiety Affects Learning

Anxiety causes learning problems in several ways. Let's first start by looking at how it affects your homework. Students with high math anxiety have difficulty starting or completing assignments. Doing homework reminds some students of their learning problems in math. More specifically, it reminds them of previous math failures, which causes further anxiety. This anxiety sometimes leads to total avoidance of homework or "approach-avoidance" behavior; students start their homework, then they quit, return later, then quit again. Total homework avoidance is called procrastination. The thought of doing homework causes these students anxiety, which then causes them to put it off. Procrastination makes them feel better for a short time — until test day.

Math anxiety also affects your classroom participation and learning. Usually students with math anxiety are afraid to speak out in class and ask questions. They are also afraid of asking a question that others, including the teacher, might consider dumb. They sit in class fearful of being asked a question, looking like they understand the lecture so they will not be called on. They also take a lot of notes, even though they don't understand them, to give the illusion of comprehension. If you are one of these students, these are hard habits to break. Still, there are numerous ways to overcome them. Here are just a few:

1. *Make an appointment to talk to your math instructor.* Math instructors want to talk to you. When I do my consulting around the country, one of the major complaints I get from math instructors is that students don't come and see them. Make an appointment to see your math instructor before the first major test to discuss your math history and to ask for suggestions.

2. *Before class, ask the instructor to work one homework problem.* Write the problem on the board before the instructor arrives. This is less stressful because you are not asking the question in front of the whole class. Choose an easy question, if possible.

3. *Prepare one question from your homework and ask it within the first 15 minutes of class.* Instructors are more likely to answer questions in the first part of class when they have time instead of the end of class when time is running out.

4. *Ask a question about a problem to which you already know the answer.* That way, if the instructor asks you a question about the problem, you will know the answer. This is good practice for asking questions about things you don't understand.

5. *Use email to send questions to your instructor.* This way you can still get the answer with very little anxiety. Do not, however, overuse this option. If you send too many emails, your instructor may begin to ignore you.

6. *Set up an appointment with your disability counselor/advisor to discuss anxiety issues.* Review your test scores from your psycho-educational report, IEP or Section 504 plan. If necessary, ask for a referral to obtain help in reducing anxiety. Do not be embarrassed. Always remember to get the help you need.

7. *Set up an appointment with your veteran advisor or certifying officer.* Discuss your test anxiety and ask for helpful resources. If you have PTSD, discuss these issues. Ask for a referral for obtain assistance.

By completing these steps, you are setting up a new history of positive expreinces. Not only will these tips help you become more comfortable in a math classroom, but they also allow you to change your overall attitude toward math. It is important to remember that math anxiety *can* be overcome with your effort. You don't have to live in the past with your math fears. Today is a new day and you can change how math affects you.

Activity 5.1 Revisiting Past Math Experiences

If you have math anxiety, try to remember the first time you had uneasy feelings about math. This does not include anxiety when taking a math test, which will be discussed later in this chapter. To help you remember this experience, check the appropriate response and answer the following questions:

1. Was your first negative math experience in:

    Elementary School   _____

    Middle School   _____

    High School   _____

    Never   _____

2. Can you recall the incident(s)?
    Yes   _____

    No   _____

3. Was it after....

    Being called on in class and getting the answer wrong?   _____

    Getting a poor grade on a homework assignment?   _____

    A parent saying he/she cannot do math and neither can you?   _____

    Another adult telling you that cannot do math?   _____

    A fellow student telling you that you are not good at math?   _____

    A teacher telling you that you are not good at math.   _____

4. If your first negative math experience is not listed above, then write it down here:

5. If you cannot remember a specific incident, then when was the last time you told yourself that you could not learn math?

    Today   _____

    Yesterday   _____

    Last Month _____

    Last Year   _____

    Never   _____

Creating Your Math Autobiography

Now that you have finished the questionnaire, it is time to start your math autobiography. The autobiography relates to how you remember and feel about past math experiences. It also helps you explore how these past feelings and events have shaped your current life. Math autobiographies are a good healing tool that help you let go of negative experiences. To find a blank form for your math autobiography, visit AcademicSuccess.com, click Student Resources and enter the following info:

Username: Wam
Password: Student

Once you have downloaded the file, print it out and get to writing! Here are a few tips to get you started:

1. When writing your math autobiography, it is easiest to start by remembering your first negative and/or positive experiences with math. You have already written a little bit about these experiences. Use Activity 5.1 as a basis for your continued writing.

2. After you have sufficiently explained these experiences, explore how they have shaped your lifelong relationship with math. There is a good chance that your initial experiences with math continue to play a huge role in your academic career. If not, don't worry. Simply write down how you have managed to persevere through bad experiences, or have used positive experiences as fuel for continued success.

3. Finally, what are your short and long term goals in terms of redefining your relationship with math? Do you want to learn to love it? Do you want to grin and bear it long enough to pass? Whatever your goals are, it is important to stay positive. Explore these questions as you draw your math autobiography to a close.

As for what to do with your finished product, you'll need to consult your current teacher or counselor. Depending on your instructor, you may be able to hand in your completed form as your autobiography. Make sure to make a personal copy before turning it in.

Even if your instructor does not require you to hand in your autobiography, it remains important to fill one out anyway. Your math autobiography is an important tool to help you become a better math student and to help reduce your math and test anxiety.

If need be, share and discuss your math autobiography with a counselor or college psychologist. They might provide you with a few great insights into your behavior. Don't be afraid to seek out the help you need.

Understanding Test Anxiety

Test anxiety has existed for as long as tests have been issued to evaluate student performance. Because it is so common, and because it has survived the test of time, test anxiety has been carefully studied over the last fifty years. Pioneering studies indicate that test anxiety generally leads to low test scores.

At the University of South Florida (Tampa), Dr. Charles Spielberger investigated the relationship between test anxiety and intellectual ability. The study results suggested that anxiety coupled with high ability can improve academic performance; but anxiety coupled with low or average ability often interferes with academic performance. That is:

Anxiety + High Ability = Improvement
Anxiety + Low or Average Ability = No Improvement

Test anxiety is a learned response brought on by environtmental conditioning. A person is not born with it. It is a special kind of general stress, or a "strained exertion," which sometimes leads to physical and psychological problems. The good news? Because test anxiety is a *learned* response, it can eventually be *unlearned* through hard work and discipline. Read on through this chapter to find out more.

Definition of Test Anxiety

According to the Diagnostic and Statistics Manual of Mental Disorders, test anxiety is characterized by an "extreme fear of poor performance on tests and examinations." The DSM goes on to describe a statistical correlation between test-anxiety and various character attributes, including but not limited to low self-esteem, dependency and passivity.

One of my students once compared test anxiety to "being in a burning house with no way out." Another described it as "a sick feeling I get on test days that makes me feel like a child and makes me forget everything."

No matter how you define it, test anxiety is real, and it affects millions of students.

The Causes of Test Anxiety

The causes of test anxiety are different for each student. The initial incident could possibly have occurred in elementary or middle school. For many students, however, test anxiety first occurs in college when passing tests is the only way to pass a course. In most college courses, homework and extra credit do not count toward your grade. Now students must have a passing average, and, in some cases, pass an intimidating departmental final exam.

Additional pressure also exists because not passing algebra means you won't graduate, and you might not get the job you want.

PTSD is another cause of test-anxiety. Students with PTSD often fear stress itself, which in turn causes a vicious loop of self-doubt, panic, and more anxiety. Many of these students are also dealing with Traumatic Brain Injuries (TBIs), which often go hand-in-hand with memory problems. Students with TBIs are often caught in a viscious loop. First, they fear that they will forget important information on test days. Then, on test day, the stress from this fear causes them to struggle, which only reinforces their initial anxiety.

Since we have already explored your experiences with general math anxiety, let's look at some of the direct causes of your math test anxiety. If you do have test anxiety, what is the main cause? If you don't know, then review the ten causes of test anxiety on this page. Does one of these reasons fit you? If you don't have test anxiety, think of scenarios that might bring it on in the future.

If you have math test anxiety, following the suggestions in this chapter and the rest of the book can greatly reduce it. The first step was already taken by understanding how you developed test anxiety. The second step is writing the reasons.

For conveinence, here is a review of the 10 basic causes of test anxiety.

1. *Test anxiety is* a learned behavior resulting from the expectations of parents, teachers or other significant people in the student's life.

2. *Test anxiety is* sometimes caused by the association between grades and a student's personal worth.

3. *Test anxiety* develops from the fear of alienating parents, family or friends due to poor grades.

4. *Test anxiety* stems from a feeling of lack of control and an inability to change one's life situation.

5. *Test anxiety* is sometimes caused by a student being embarrassed by the teacher or other students when trying to do math problems.

6. *Test anxiety* often occurs during timed tests due to the fear of not finishing the test. This is true even when a student is capable of doing all of the problems.

7. *Test anxiety* is sometimes caused by being put in math courses that are above the student's level of competence.

8. *Students leaving* the room before the test time is up often triggers anxiety among the remaining students.

9. *PTSD* often triggers test-anxiety.

10. *TBIs* often trigger test-anxiety.

The Different Types of Test Anxiety

The two basic types of test anxiety are *emotional* ("somatic") and *worry* ("cognitive"). Students with high test anxiety have both emotional and worry anxiety.

Signs of emotional anxiety are upset stomach, nausea, sweaty palms, pain in the neck, stiff shoulders, high blood pressure, rapid shallow breathing, rapid heartbeat or general feelings of nervousness. As anxiety increases, these feelings intensify.

Even though these feelings are caused by anxiety, the physical response is real. These feelings and physical inconveniences affect your concentration and your testing speed, and sometimes cause you to "draw a blank."

Worry anxiety causes students to think about failing a test. This negative "self-talk" causes students to focus on their anxiety instead of recalling math concepts by telling themselves that they will fail the test. This talk is perhaps the worst enemy of a math student. Not only does it reinforce bad behavior, it also prohibits a student from establishing positive energy. Negative self-statements vary from student to student.

Students with worry anxiety have told me many things after not being able to solve problems:

- "What is wrong with me?"
- "I did these types of problems before."
- "I just cannot get math!"
- "Math is awful!"
- "I hate math!"
- "I don't need it for my career so why am I taking the course."
- "I am going to fail this test and this course."
- "I might as well drop this course and quit college."
- "I am dumb."

These types of statements cause more worry anxiety and divert your attention away from the test, leaving you less time to complete problems. Later on in the chapter we discuss how to get rid of these types of statements.

Students may have different levels of emotional anxiety and worry anxiety. The treatment depends on the levels of your type of test anxiety. All students have a total test anxiety level, a emotional anxiety level and a worry level. On a scale of 1 to 100, determine your self-reported total anxiety, worry anxiety and emotional anxiety. A level of 1 means no anxiety, a level of 50 means average anxiety and a level of 100 means the highest anxiety (meaning you cannot even walk in the room during test day without getting sick). Students usually have different anxiety levels in all three categories. Below, fill in the numbers that represent your levels.

Emotional anxiety _____

Worry anxiety _____

Total anxiety _____

Low levels of anxiety are between 1 and 25. Moderate low levels of anxiety are between 26 and 50. Moderately high levels of anxiety are between 51 and 75. High levels of anxiety fall between 76 and 99. Based on this information you can change your score.

What is your highest area of anxiety? Students who have high test anxiety have both emotional and worry anxiety.

The Effects of Anxiety on Testing and Learning

The effects of anxiety on student learning and testing can best be explained by looking at the Stages of Memory process (Chapter Six). The Stages of Memory are Sensory Input, Sensory Register, Short-term Memory, Working Memory, Abstract Reasoning, Long-term Memory and Memory Output.

When anxious students read a math textbook or learn mathematics in the classroom, their anxiety can affect their Sensory Register and Short-term Memory. Anxiety interferes with how fast people process information and can decrease the amount of information they can hold for a short period of time. This means that less information enters Working Memory, which is where mathematics information is combined and learned.

Also, anxiety mainly affects Working Memory by decreasing the amount of information that can be processed at the same time. This leads to poor Memory Output such as not understanding what you read or not answering a question during class.

Example: Anxiety manifests itself differently in every student. The effects of test anxiety range from a "mental block" on a test to avoidance of homework. These symptoms also range in severity.

The most recent research indicates that test anxiety strongly affects Working Memory. Authors Ashcraft and Kirk (2001) indicate that math anxiety temporarily disrupts mental processing in Working Memory that causes poorer math achievement. Math anxiety uses up Working Memory resources that make it harder to learn math. During tests, math test anxiety decreases the amount of Working Memory space, which means less information can be received and used from Long-term Memory and Abstract Reasoning. This is like using a calculator in which half of the keys are not functioning. The result is a slow down in performance and a decrease in accuracy, resulting in poorer grades.

One of the most common side effects of test anxiety is getting the test and immediately forgetting information that you know. Some students describe this event as having a "mental block," "going blank," or indicating that the test looks like Greek. After five or ten minutes into the test, some of these students can refocus and start working the problems. They have, however, lost valuable time.

For other students, anxiety persists throughout the test and they cannot recall the needed information. It is only after they walk out the door that they can remember how to work the problems. When this happens, they get mad at themselves, which increases their fears that the same thing will happen on the next test.

Sometimes students with math test anxiety do not "go blank," but it takes longer to recall formulas and concepts and to work problems. The result is frustration and loss of time, leading to more anxiety.

Since, in most cases, math tests are speed tests (those in which you have a certain amount of time to complete the test), you may not have enough time to work all the problems or to check the answers if you have mentally slowed down. The result is a lower test score because even though you knew the material, you did not complete all of the questions before the test time ran out.

Not using all of the time allotted for the test is another problem caused by test anxiety. This is particularly frustrating, because this behavior is entirely avoidable. Most students know that they should use all of their test time to check their answers. In fact, math is one of the few subjects in which you can check test problems to find out if you have

the problems correct. However, most students do not use all of their given test time, and this results in lower test scores.

Why? Students with high test anxiety do not want to stay in the classroom. This is especially true of students whose test anxiety increases as a test progresses. Test anxiety gets so bad in these situations that some students are willing to get a bad grade just to leave the classroom a little bit early.

Even more common among anxious students is the fear of what the instructor and other students will think about them for being the last one to hand in a test. These students refuse to be in the last group to finish, because they feel the instructor or other students will think they are dumb.

This is middle-school thinking, but the feelings are still real — no matter the age of the student. These students do not realize that some students who turn in their tests first fail, while many students who turn in their tests last make "A's" and "B's." Assumptions in this regard are extremely detrimental toward making good grades.

When taking a test, you need to focus on yourself and yourself only. Do not worry about what your classmates are doing. Instead, keep your eyes on your own test and imagine the relief you will feel when you hand in your test confident that you did not make any careless errors.

Another effect of test anxiety relates to completing homework assignments. Students who have high test anxiety often have difficulty starting or completing homework. The material on the homework causes them to think about previous tests or begin worrying about the next test and whether they are going to stress out in front of their classmates.

Some students begin their homework and work some problems successfully. They then get stuck on a problem that causes them anxiety, so they take a break. During their break the anxiety disappears until they start doing their homework again. Doing their homework causes more anxiety, which leads to another break. The breaks become more frequent. Finally, the student takes one long break and does not do the homework. Quitting, to them, means no more anxiety until the next homework assignment.

The effects of math test anxiety can be different for each student. Students can have several of the mentioned characteristics that can interfere with math learning and test taking. Remember, many popular conceptions about test anxiety are entirely inaccurate. Review the 12 Myths About Test Anxiety chart, printed to the right, to see which ones you believe.

It is important to stick to the information in this book and not fall victim to advice from well-meaning but uninformed friends. Test anxiety is a very real problem and cannot be cured by simply disregarding its existence.

Now that we understand how math anxiety and math test anxiety affect learning and testing, it is time to learn how to reduce your test anxiety. The first step to doing this is to remain positve. Tell yourself, "I can reduce my math test anxiety. It may take some time, but I *can* reduce my math test anxiety."

Attitudes Toward Tests

Your attitude toward tests is extremely important before and after tests. Some students see tests as a necessary evil. Others see them as an opportunity to demonstrate knowledge. Most maintain attitudes that fall somewhere between these two. In truth, tests are neither good nor bad—they are simply a tool to measure your knowledge.

It is important that you, as a student, understand this. Tests are just a highway sign directing you toward your goals. Even if you veer off the road on one test, you can immediately get help from a tutor, a classmate, or an instructor to get you back on track. In this way, minor detours aren't a big deal. If anything, they'll inspire you to perform better, as well as finally get the sort of assistance that'll help you long term.

Don't take tests personally. Doing poorly on a test doesn't mean that you are a bad person, nor does doing well on a test make

12 Myths About Test Anxiety

1. Students are born with test anxiety.

2. Test anxiety is a mental illness.

3. Test anxiety cannot be reduced.

4. Any level of test anxiety is bad.

5. All students who are not prepared will have test anxiety.

6. Students with test anxiety cannot learn math.

7. Students who are well prepared will not have test anxiety.

8. Very intelligent students and students taking high-level courses, such as calculus, do not have test anxiety.

9. Attending class and doing my homework should reduce all of my test anxiety.

10. Being told to relax during a test will make you relaxed.

11. Doing nothing about test anxiety will make it go away.

12. Reducing test anxiety will guarantee better grades.

you a good person. This may sound like an exaggeration, but I have known countless students who have viewed themselves as one or the other after taking tests. To think this way is a waste of time. Your self-worth does not depend on making good test grades.

Again, it's important to use mindfulness to improve your attitude toward tests. This will help you regulate your emotions. Don't think about what has happened during past tests or what you think might happen in the future. Stay in the moment and think positively about the current test you are taking and how it can help you accomplish your goals. Mindfulness really works when you practice and apply it. Don't be afraid to try it out!

Activity 5.2 Revisiting Past Test Experiences

If you have test anxiety, try to remember the first time you had uneasy feelings about taking a math test. To help you remember this experience, check the appropriate response and answer the questions:

Was your first negative test experience in:

Elementary School _____

Middle School   _____

High School   _____

1. Can you recall the incident(s)?

    Yes   _____

    No   _____

2. Was it after....

    Your first alegbra test? _____

    Your first math test after being out of school for a long time? _____

    After you decided to get serious about college? _____

    When a professor told you that you needed to pass a test to pass a course? _____

    When you needed to pass a test to maintain your financial aid? _____

    After a parent asked you why you failed a previous test? _____

    Your children asking you why you failed your last test? _____

    If your first negative test experience is not listed above, then write it down here:

    If you cannot remember a specific incident when you had test anxiety, do you expect to have any major test anxiety on your next math test? If so, write down your situation below:

How to Reduce Math and Test Anxiety

To reduce math and test anxiety, you need to understand both the relaxation response and how negative self-talk undermines your abilities. These anxiety reduction techniques and positive self-statements can be used before or during your homework, class or test. These techniques need to be practiced several times before they become effective. If you have extremely high test anxiety, you need to practice long-term relaxation techniques. This mainly involves learning how to turn negative self-talk statements into positive self-talk statements.

Short-Term Relaxation Techniques

The relaxation response is any technique or procedure that helps you to become relaxed and takes the place of an anxiety response. There are both short-term and long-term relaxation response techniques, which help control emotional math test anxiety.

These techniques also help reduce worry anxiety. Among others, effective short-term techniques include the Tensing and Differential Relaxation Method and the Palming Method. The next four subsections describe these methods in further detail. Try them all to figure out which works best for you.

Tensing & Relaxing Method

The Tensing and Relaxation Method helps you relax by tensing and relaxing your muscles all at once. Follow these procedures while sitting at your desk before taking a test:

1. *Put your* feet flat on the floor.
2. *Grab underneath* your chair with your hands.
3. *Push down* with your feet and *pull up* on your chair at the same time for about five seconds.
4. *Relax* for five to ten seconds.
5. *Repeat the procedure* two to three times.
6. *Relax all your muscles* except the ones that are actually used to take the test.

Deep Breathing Technique

Deep Breathing is a technique that can reduce your test anxiety. Follow these steps to Deep Breathing:

1. *Inhale slowly* and deeply through your nose by filling up the bottom of your lungs first.

2. *Stop* for a few seconds and hold your breath.

3. *Exhale slowly* through your mouth pretending like you are whistling out the air. Be sure to exhale fully and let your whole body relax. Wait a few seconds and then start to inhale as stated in number 1.

After practicing deep breathing it should become a very natural process. You may want to repeat the steps five times and then take a break. You may then want to do one more set.

If you start to get light-headed while practicing, stop for a few minutes. You were probably breathing in and out too fast. Practicing this breathing technique will make it easier to use before or during the test if needed. This technique will help some students to relax, while other students may prefer other short-term techniques.

Visualization

Have you ever daydreamed in class or during a workshop? I have asked this question to thousands of students and the answer is always yes. Then I ask them what happens when they daydream. The answer is that their minds leave the room and the body thinks it is where the mind has gone. Then I ask what would happen if you daydreamed about some relaxing place? Your mind would tell your body to relax. This process is called visualization, or using visual images in your mind to reduce test anxiety.

This technique has been used for hundreds of years. Athletes also use this technique to reduce their anxiety and to improve their game performance. You can imagine anything or anyplace in order to reduce your test anxiety. Follow these steps to practice visualization:

1. *Find a comfortable place to sit.*

2. *Close your eyes and think* about a relaxing place, real or imaginary.

3. *Imagine yourself in that place*, making sure to *see* it through your own eyes, not seeing yourself from afar.

4. *Make the scene as real as possible.* What type of sounds do you *hear*? What do you *smell*? Are you feeling the sand between your toes or maybe the cool air?

5. *Visualize that scene* for one to two minutes.

6. *Open your eyes* and continue to feel relaxed.

Suggestion: Develop two scenes and practice them every day until you can relax yourself in a few minutes. Then you will be ready to use them on the test.

Palming Method

The palming method is a visualization procedure used to reduce test anxiety. While you are at your desk before or during a test, follow these procedures:

1. *Close* and *cover your eyes* using the the palms of your hands.

2. *Do not rub or touch your eyeballs. Prevent your hands* from touching your eyes by resting the lower parts of your palms on your cheeks and placing your fingers on your forehead.

3. *Think of some real or imaginary scenes*-that are relaxing to you.

4. *Visualize this scene.* Picture it as if you were actually there. Do this for one to two minutes.

Practice visualizing this scene several days before taking a test and the effectiveness of this relaxation procedure will improve.

Long-Term Relaxation Techniques

The Cue-Controlled Relaxation Response Technique is the best long-term relaxation technique. Cue-Controlled Relaxation works by inducing your own relaxation based on repeating certain cue words to yourself. In essence, you are taught to relax and then silently repeat cue words, such as "I am relaxed." After enough practice, you can relax during math tests. To practice these techniques, talk to your advisor for resources or see Web-Based Text Anxiety Reduction (Nolting, 2012).

Managing Self-Talk

Imagine two students taking their first math test during the semester, and half way through the exam they start missing several problems. One student starts saying to himself that he is going to fail the test and might as well turn in his paper and quit. The other student says: "I might miss these problems but that is not a reason to give up and leave. I will just try as hard as I can on the other problems and I can pass."

One student feels anxiety and the other student remains calm and develops a plan. In both cases, the situation is the same, but the feelings in response to the test situation are extremely different due to their internal dialogue or self-talk. Which student are you?

Cognitive psychologists claim that what we say to ourselves in a response to an event mainly determines our mood or feeling about that event. Sometimes we say these statements to ourselves so quickly and automatically that we don't even notice. We then believe the situation is causing the feeling, when it is actually our interactions or thoughts about the event that are controlling our emotions.

This sequence is represented by the following timeline:

External Events (Math Test)

Interpretation of Events with Self-Talk

Feelings, Emotions and Reactions

Based on this psychological theory, in most cases you are responsible for what you feel. You have a choice to have positive or negative self-talk while doing your math homework or during a math test. This can determine how you feel during the test and control some of your anxiety. Some students see a math test as an opportunity to show their knowledge of the subject and are excited about that, while others see the same test as a potential failure that will lead to anger and dissatisfaction. The realization that you are responsible for your own feelings is very powerful once you fully accept it. Some points about self-talk include:

- Self-Talk is like a telegraphic message where one or two words can bring up many different thoughts and feelings.

- Self-Talk is like a looped audio recording, repeating the same words.

- Self–Talk happens automatically. You don't even think about what you are saying to yourself.

- Negative self-talk during anxious situations is usually illogical, though it might seem rational at the time.

- Positive self-talk can increase appropriate behavior. Telling yourself that you can do your homework can lead to actually doing your homework.

- Negative self-talk causes avoidance and procrastination. Students who tell themselves they are not good in math don't want to do their homework and avoid it whenever possible.

Negative Self-Talk

Students who have high test anxiety usually use negative self-talk. This negative self-talk can increase the student's test anxiety and may cause them to fail. It is totally possible for students with negative self-talk to change this bad habit.

To change the negative self-talk habit, it is beneficial to understand the different types of negative self-talk. If you have negative self-talk, then review the different types to see which one matches you best. You may be one type or a combination of different types.

The Worrier — Worriers always look for the worst-case situation. They are scared of failure. When they feel a little bit of anxiety, they blow it out of proportion and give up, believing there is nothing that can help them pass. In some extreme cases, they drop out of college believing they will never be able to pass a math course. The worrier's favorite question is, "What if . . . ?" For example, "What if I fail this test and then this class? I will not graduate and be in this dead-end job forever or all my friends will make fun of me." The Worrier can eventually give in to fear and sabotage his/herself in self-defense from disappointment.

The Victim — "Victims" want to feel helpless and hopeless. They create anxiety by telling themselves that no matter what they do, they will not be successful in math. Victims believe there is something wrong with them that is not curable. They do not blame other factors that they can change, such as decreasing anxiety and improving their math study skills. They want to doom themselves and get into a learned helplessness mode that eventually stops them from even trying. They grow accustom to failure. The Victim's favorite statement is, "I can't. I will never be able to no matter how hard I try . . ."

The Critic — Critics like to put themselves down. They look for internal flaws, and if

Negative self-talk causes students to behave in a counterproductive manner. A proper self-esteem is required for success in math classes.

they don't have any, they create some. They put themselves down when they notice other students not showing any anxiousness. They ignore their success, and instead of being proud of their accomplishments, they believe them to be a fluke. The Critic's favorite statement is, "You are too stupid to learn math!" If Critics do pass a test, they say afterward, "You could have made a better grade. Look at all those careless errors." The Critic's goal is to promote low self-esteem so that he or she will stop learning math. This behavior is disasterous come grade time. More often than not, it leads to failure.

The Perfectionist

Perfectionists are closely related to Critics, but instead of putting themselves down for missing problems, they use the experience to push themselves toward success.

Perfectionists cannot stand mistakes or poor grades. They drive themselves to exhaustion making sure they understand every single concept. Self-worth means nothing to them because they will never be happy with anything less than perfection. This eventually leads to failure when they pass their "breaking point." Even a grade such as a 92 is not good enough. In some cases, it drives them toward causing harm to themselves.

Do any of these sound familiar?

After reading about these different types of personalities, which one can you most relate to? The person inside of you may be a combination of two different types, but there usually is one personality that dominates your perception of math. Once again, do not beat yourself up if you fall into one of these categories. In fact, just about everybody exhibits signs of at least one category. With this in mind, the next step is to learn how to cope with these problems, as well as how to begin using your personality type to become successful.

Positive Self-Talk

You can counter and control negative self-talk in several ways. Negative self-talk is easily replaced with positive self-talk. You can also develop thought-stopping techniques that reduce negative self-talk and engender positive self-talk.

Try all of the following ways to discover which one, or combination of two techniques, work best for you. The first technique is to develop positive self-talk statements. The following list of suggestions will help you develop a series of personal statements, which you should memorize as soon as possible.

1. *Use the first person perspective.* For example, "I can control my anxiety and pass this test."

2. *Avoid using negatives in the statement.* For example, don't say, "I will not get nervous during this test." Instead say, "I will calm myself down during the test.

3. *Make the statements positive and realistic.* For example, you can say, "I will be successful on this test", instead of saying, "I will make a 100 on this test."

The Worrier, who asks, "What if I fail the test?" can counter with, "If I fail the test I will just do better on the next one."

The Victim, who believes things are hopeless says: "No way will I ever pass math." They can counter with: "I used a different way to study and take the test so I can pass the course this time."

The Critic, who puts themselves down by saying: "I cannot reduce my test anxiety and will fail." They can replace this by saying: "I know I have test anxiety but I have learned to control it."

The Perfectionist, who says, "I must make an A or I am a failure," can instead say, "I don't need an A to be successful. I just need to pass this course so I can take the next one and graduate."

These are examples of positive self-talk that can control anxiety. Additional positive self-talk statements are listed below.

- "I failed the course last semester, but I can now use my math study skills to pass this course."

- "I went blank on the last test, but I now know how to reduce my test anxiety."

- "I know that my poor math skills are due to poor study skills, not my own ability, and since I am working on my study skills, my math skills will improve."

- "I know that, with hard work, I will pass math."

- "I prepared for this test and will do

the best I can. I will reduce my test anxiety and use the best test-taking procedures. I expect some problems will be difficult, but I will not get discouraged."

Create your own positive self-talk statements in Activity 5.3, which is found at the end of this section.

Thought-Stopping Technique

Many students have difficulty controlling their negative self-talk. These students have tried to tell themselves to eliminate the negative self-talk, but no matter what they try it persists. These students need a thought-stopping technique to break this bad habit.

Thought-stopping entails focusing on unwanted negative self-talk, and then suddenly stopping those thoughts with some type of internal or external action. Actions such as yelling to yourself, "Stop that," or making a loud noise, such as slapping a desk, effectively interrupt negative self-talk.

Obviously, your location plays a role in what you should and should not do. In a homework situation, you may want to slap the desk, but obviously doing this in a crowded classroom is inappropriate.

To stop your negative thoughts in a crowded classroom, while listening to a lecture, or while during a test, silently shout to yourself, "Stop thinking about that." After your silent shout, either relax yourself or repeat one of the positive self-talk statements that you have made up. You may have to shout to yourself several times to control your negative self-talk. After every shout, use a different relaxation technique, such as positive visual scenes or positive statements that will help control your anxiety.

The way "stop-thinking" works is by interrupting the worry response before it creates the type of anxiety that gets out of control. During the interruptions, you gain control and replace negative self-talk with positive responses. Students with high worry anxiety need to practice these techniques at

least one week before a test several times a day. Then, they need to keep practicing once a day until the negative self-talk completely disappears.

If needed, obtain additional help from your counselor or college psychologist to help you stop negative self-talk. Doing so prepares you to deal with inevitable adversity and sets you on the right path toward a positive math attitude.

Power of Positive Thinking

If you remain skeptical about the power of positive thinking, here is one more fact to persuade you. According to a 1985 study, conducted by psychologists Michael Scheier and Charles Carver (1985), optimists are much more likely to succeed in life, largely because they are more capable of coping with adversity. When they are presented with challenges, optimists manage to navigate through their negative feelings and ultimately persevere. The benefits of being an optimist don't stop there. They also live longer and sustain better overall mental and physical health than do pessimists.

Mindfulness

Another great technique to reduce anxiety involves the "Mindfulness" techniques mentioned in Chapter One. If you remember, mindfulness is the ability to interact with the present moment with full attention, without allowing thoughts, internal dialogue, and accompanying emotions to interfere with how we interact in the present.

In many ways, mindfulness is just another way to ensure that you maintain a happy and healthy relationship with your high school/college experience. Oddly, graduates often look back fondly at stressful tests. Eventually these tests become war stories: the sort a person often embellishes to either get a laugh or paint a vivid picture of a difficult course. By staying in the moment, you can appreciate stressful times as being part of the overall excitement of being in college.

Activity 5.3 Creating Positive Self-Talk Statements

As you've just read, in order to succeed in a math class, you must replace negative self-talk statements with positive self-talk statements. Now that you've read the instructions in this chapter, you can go ahead and develop your positive self-talk statements in the space below. Develop four positive self-talk statements that are not in this book, making sure to use the word "I "in each statement.

Statement 1:

Statement 2:

Statement 3:

Statement 4:

Why Doing Your Homework and Attending Class May Not Be Enough to Pass

Taking a math test is different from taking tests in other subjects. First, math tests not only require you to recall information, but apply it as well. Second, math tests build on each other, requiring students to know and recall material from previous units. Third, most math tests are speed tests. Fourth, computer-based learning and online tests have strict time restraints and in most cases you cannot go back and review the problems.

During a test, your working memory pulls information from your long-term memory and/or fluid reasoning areas. It then puts this information together in order to answer questions. At the same time you are reading the problems, your brain is also deciding how to progress through the test, calculating answers and performing other functions. All this work requires working memory space, so you need to develop test-taking strategies and use accommodations if appropriate to free up enough working memory to correctly solve problems. Remember, math test preparation and test-taking skills are different from those needed for tests in other subjects. You need to have a test-taking plan to demonstrate your total knowledge. Students with these plans make better grades than their peers.

Most students and some instructors believe that attending class and completing every homework assignment ensures an "A" or "B" on tests. This is far from true. Listening in class and understanding how to solve problems at home is very different from actually solving the problems on a test.

Here are the reasons why:

1. In class, instructors can ask you questions to lead you to the next step.

2. In class, instructors can give you hints to help solve problems.

3. In class, you can ask helpful questions.

4. In class, instructors can do all the problem steps for you.

5. In class, you can refer to your textbook or solution manual.

6. In small groups, other students can help you solve problems.

7. There is less anxiety solving problems in class than during a test.

8. If you do not learn how to solve a problem in class, you can go to the instructor or tutor afterwards.

9. While in an Emporium model classroom, homework management systems feature help buttons, which refer you to text sections and videos.

10. While in an online class, you can email the instructor or Google results.

Many students get a false sense of security because they know how to do the math problems while in class or when doing online homework. Then, when the test comes around, they have difficulty solving the same problems. Don't let this happen to you! I have worked with hundreds of students who falsely assume that they understand how to solve math problems because they got all the homework problems correct weeks before taking a test. These students guessed their way into failure, because they did not truly understand important math concepts. They did not take any notes on the problems they missed to review before the test. This reviewing could have moved the information from working memory to long-term memory or fluid reasoning. Correctly answering homework problems is very different from taking tests:

1. While doing homework there is little anxiety.

2. You are not under a time constraint while doing your homework.

3. If you get stuck on a homework problem, you have your textbook and notes.

4. Once you learn how to do several problems in a homework assignment, the rest are similar.

5. In doing homework, you have the answers to at least half the problems in the back of the text and can use apps to solve problems.

6. While doing homework, you have time to figure out how to correctly use your calculator.

7. When doing homework, you can call your study buddy or ask a tutor for help.

8. When doing your homework, you can go to the Web and find online tutoring.

9. While in a Emporium model classroom, the homework management program gives you hints, examples and answers.

10. While in an online class, you can access online live tutor support programs, such as Smart Thinking.

General Pre-Test Rules

1. *Get a good night's sleep before taking a test.* If you cram all night and imagine you will perform well on your test with three to four hours of sleep, you are wrong. It is better to get seven or eight hours sleep and be fresh enough to use your memory to recall information needed to answer the questions.

2. *Start studying for the test at least three days ahead of time.* Make sure you take a practice test to find out what you do not know. Review and work the problems in your problem log. If you did not do a problem log, use the chapter review test to find out what you don't know. An even better way is to work with classmates to make up test questions. Review the concept errors you made on the last test. Meet with your instructor or tutor for help on those questions you cannot solve.

3. *Only review already-learned material the night before a test.* This prevents you from forgetting information. Studying new material sometimes forces learned concepts out of your memory.

4. *Make sure you know all the information on your mental cheat sheet.* Review your notebook to make sure you understand the concepts. Work a few problems and recall the information on your mental cheat sheet right before you go to bed. Go directly to bed; do not watch television, listen to the radio or view social media. While you are asleep, your mind works on and remembers the last thing you did before going to bed.

5. *Get up in the morning at your usual time and review your notes and problem log.* Do not do any new problems. Make sure your calculator is working.

Ten Steps to Better Classroom Math Test-Taking

Most students know how to take a multiple choice test, but have no clue about the best way to take a math test. When taking any test, you are being measured in two areas: the content of the material and how well you take a test. To take a math test you need a plan. This plan will make you more efficient and confident. The plan needs to be developed before you take the test and needs to be followed during the test. I have known hundreds of students who have lost tests points because they did not have a test plan and did not practice that plan before taking the test. Make sure you develop and memorize your mental cheat sheet so you can write down the information on the test (don't use the sheet during the test). Finally, make sure to practice the test-taking steps printed below.

10 Steps to Taking a Math Test (in class)

The following few pages describe a math test-taking method that has help thousands of students thrive in their math courses. Before reading the steps, however, you need to assess your current test taking method. To do this, complete activity 5.4, which is located on page 131. If you are currently taking an online math course, fill out the same form and move on to the "10 Steps to Better Online Test-Taking" section in this chapter.

Step One — *Use a memory data dump.* When you get your test, turn it over and write down the information that you put on your mental cheat sheet. Your mental cheat sheet has now turned into a mental list and writing down this information is not cheating. Do not put your name on the test, do not skim it, just turn it over and write down those facts, figures and formulas from your mental cheat sheet or other information you might not remember during the test. This is called your first memory data dump. The data dump provides memory cues for test questions.

Step Two — *Preview the test.* Put your name on the test and start previewing. Look through the entire test to find different types of problems and their point values.

Put a mark by the questions that you can do without thinking. These are the questions that you will solve first.

Step Three — *Do a second memory data dump.*

The second data dump is for writing down material that was jarred from your memory while previewing the test. Write this information on the back of the test.

Step Four — *Develop a test progress schedule.*

When you begin setting up a test schedule, determine the point value for each question. You might have some test questions that are worth more points than others. In some tests, word problems are worth five points and other questions might be worth two or three points. Just like in a video game, you must decide the best way to get the most points in the least amount of time. This might mean working the questions worth two to three points first and leaving the more difficult word problems for last. Decide how many problems should be completed halfway through the test. You should have more than half the problems completed by that time.

Step Five — *Answer the easiest problems first.*

Solve, in order, the problems you marked while previewing the test. Then, review the answers to see if they make sense. Start working through the test as fast as you can while being accurate. Answers should be reasonable. For example, the answer to a problem of trying to find the area of a rectangle cannot be negative, and the answer to a land-rate-distance problem cannot be 1,000 miles per hour. Clearly write down each step to get partial credit, even if you end up missing the problem. In most math tests, the easier problems are near the beginning of the first page; you need to answer them efficiently and quickly. Completing several easy problems first boosts your confidence, decreases anxiety and guarantees test points.

Step Six — *Complete the difficult problems you know how to do.*

These are the problems that have quite a few steps and take some time to complete, but are also problems you can complete without any real trouble. These problems are usually worth more points than the rest of the test, so it is important to finish them before you attempt problems that you don't know how to do. By finishing these problems early on in your test time, you can relax, knowing that you already have quite a few points in the bag. This will boost your confidence as you head into the problems you might not know how to do.

Step Seven — *Tackle the toughest problems.*

These are the problems that you might remember a few things about, but you don't know enough to complete them. You might remember the first step, but then draw a blank on what to do next. It is important to begin the problem, even if you know that you cannot complete it. By starting the problem and writing down what you know, you are warming up your brain, which might trigger the "Ah ha!" response. The "Ah ha!" response is when your brain suddenly remembers how to complete a problem. A memory from your homework or a lecture sometimes will pop back into your head right when you need it most. Take some time on these problems, but move on if you are completely stuck.

Step Eight — *Guess at the remaining problems.*

Do as much work as you can on each problem, even if it is just writing down the first step. If you cannot write down the first step, rewrite the problem. Also remember that the way you learned how to solve a problem was by writing, not just looking at the problem. Sometimes rewriting the problem jars your memory enough to do the first step or the entire problem. If you leave the problem blank, you will get a zero. You MUST put something down, even if it doesn't make sense. Your instructor may give you points just for the attempt.

Step Nine—*Review the test.* Look for careless errors or other errors you may have made. Students usually lose two to five test points on errors that could have been caught in review. Do not talk yourself out of an answer just because it may not look right. This often happens when an answer does not come out even. It is possible for the answer to be a fraction or a decimal. Remember, answers to math problems do not have "dress codes." Research shows that the odds of changing a right answer to a wrong one are much greater than the odds of changing a wrong answer to a right one.

Step Ten—*Use all of your alloted test time.* Review each problem by substituting the answer back into the equation or doing the opposite function required to answer the question. If you cannot check the problem in these ways, rework the problem on a separate sheet of paper and compare the answers. Do not leave the classroom unless you have reviewed each problem two times or until the bell rings or the class ends.

Even though we encourage students to work until the end of the test period, most students leave the classroom before the end of the period. These students state that even though they know they should use all their test time, they cannot stay in the room until the end of the test time. After talking to hundreds of these students, I discovered two different themes for leaving the classroom early. First, test anxiety gets so overwhelming that they cannot stay in the room. The relief from the test anxiety (leaving the room) is worth more than getting a better grade. The other reason for leaving the test early is that they do not want to be the last or one of the last few students to turn in their tests. They still believe that students who turn their tests in last are "dumb and stupid." These students also believe that students who turn their tests in first make "A's" and "B's" and those students who turn their tests in last make "D's" and "F's."

These students need a new strategy for the middle or last part of a test. This involves performing a second relaxation technique either in the middle of the test or before reviewing the problems. Students who do a short-term relaxation technique, such as visual imagery, prevent their anxiety from getting so high that they have to leave the room. Other students may do a cognitive technique, such as telling themselves to calm down, stay in the room and finish checking their answers. Students who have extremely high test anxiety can do these techniques during the middle of the test and at the end of the test to take control of their anxiety.

If you are one of these students, you don't need to care about what other students think about you (it's usually wrong anyway). YOU need to fight the urge to leave early and use all the test time. Remember, passing mathematics is the best way to get a high paying job and support yourself or your family. Do not worry about what others think. DO IT NOW!

Benefits to Turning in Your Scratch Paper

Stapling your scratch paper to a math test when handing it in has several advantages. First, if you incorrectly copy the answer from the scratch paper, you might still get partial credit for your answers.

Second, if you get the answer wrong due to a careless error, your work on the scratch paper may salvage you a few points. Third, if you do get the problem wrong, it'll be easier to locate errors when the instructor reviews the test. This prevents you from making the same mistakes on your next math test.

Fourth, showing your work proves you put in the effort to solve a problem and did not guess or leave it blank. Many professors are more generous than you'd think. If they can tell you put in the work, they may give you enough points to pass a test you might have otherwise failed. Even if you occasionally come up short, you'll never embarrass yourself if put in the right amount of work.

Activity 5.4   Assessing Your Test-Taking Methods

By reviewing how you took your last math test we can determine what changes you can make to improve your test-taking skills. In the space below, list your typical test-taking steps and explain them. Some students may have less than six steps and others may have more than six steps. If you have more than six steps, add them in the blank space at the bottom of this page.

Step One:

Step Two:

Step Three:

Step Four:

Step Five:

Step Six:

How to Become a Better Computer-Based Test Taker

Taking a computer-based math test differs in many ways from taking tests in traditional classrooms. Whether a part of an online math course or a computer-based learning course, computer-based tests usually measure two areas: the content of the material and how well you take a test. The second measure is more important for online tests than classroom tests and requires different test-taking skills.

First of all, depending on the rules and setup of the software you are using, you may have to vary your plan of attack. Different tests allow you different amounts of time to complete problems. Also, some tests allow you to revisit previous questions and some don't. I've worked with many students who have lost test points because a test was turned off after 55 minutes, and they were still working on problems. I've seen others lose points because the software prevented them from going back and checking their answers.

Before deciding which of the Ten Steps to Computer Test-Taking you want to use, ask your instructor these questions: Where can I find a hard copy of sample practice problems or a practice test? How much time do I have for the quiz or test? How many problems are on the quiz or test? Will the quiz or test automatically terminate after a certain period of time? Can I have extra test time if I did not finish a problem? Can I go back and review the problems that I do not finish? Can I go back and review the problems that I finish? Can I turn in my scratch paper for partial credit? Once the tests starts, can I use a blank sheet of paper for my memory data dump (mental cheat sheet)? After the test is graded, can I go over the test to review my mistakes?

Each instructor in a distance-learning class or Emporium model class may set up the testing process differently. Emporium tests may or may not occur during class time. It is important that you understand how this process works during the first week. It is possible that you may not be able to take the tests in the way that they are set up. Math tests in distance-learning classes have been particularly problematic. Review the syllabus to see how and where you will be tested.

In most cases, you will take practice tests and quizzes online, but the major tests will probably be in a secure test center, usually on a college campus. In some cases you may have to go to the local community college or university and pay to take the test in their testing centers. Make sure you are able to do this if it is the way the test administration is set up. If you can't, talk to the instructor immediately during the first week of classes. This way, if there are no alternative ways to take tests, you are still allowed to drop or change sections of the math class.

10 Steps to Taking a Computer-Based Math Test

Before taking your test, practice the steps listed below.

Step One — *When you get your test, use the blank sheet of paper you showed to your instructor, and write down the information from your mental cheat sheet.* Your mental cheat sheet has now turned into a list, and writing down this information is not cheating. Do not wait until you get stuck on a problem before writting down the memory data dump. By that time, you may have forgotten the information you tried to memorize. Write down facts, figures and formulas from your mental cheat sheet or other information you might not remember during the test.

Step Two — *Develop a test progress schedule.* When you begin setting up your test schedule, determine how much time you have for each question. You should already know how many questions are on the quiz or test. Then, figure out how many minutes you have to complete each problem. For example, if you have 25 test problems to complete in 60 minutes, then you have about two minutes per problem. Decide how many problems should be completed halfway through the test. You should have more than half the problems completed by that time.

Step Three — *Start by answering the problems in proper order, unless your program allows you to skip and return to problems.* Solve the problems quickly and accurately. Then, review the answers to see if they make sense. On most computer math tests, the easier problems are near the beginning; you need to answer them efficiently and quickly. This will give you more time for the harder problems and time to review the whole test (if the software allows). If you can choose the order you answer questions, always do the easiest problems first.

Step Four — *Start working through the rest of the test as fast as you can while remaining accurate and thoughtful.* Answers should be reasonable. Make sure you are using scratch paper to work problems. Clearly write down each step because if you are allowed to turn in your scratch paper, you may get partial credit even if you end up missing the problem. Also, if you cannot turn in the scratch paper with the test, you can still use the scratch paper when reviewing. This allows you to discover your mistakes and correct them.

Step Five — *Second memory data dump.* The second data dump is for writing down material that was forgotten or jarred while working on other problems. If you are working on a problem and remember something you forgot to write on your memory data dump, write it down now. If you wait to finish the problem, you may forget it.

Step Six — *Try difficult problems.* As you are working through your test, you may encounter a difficult problem. These are the problems that you might remember something about, but you don't know enough to solve them. You might remember the first step, but then draw a blank on what to do next. It is important to begin the problem, even if you know that you cannot complete it. By starting the problem and writing down what you know, you are warming up your brain, which may lead to the solution. Take time on these problems. If you get stuck and are able to return to unsolved problems, write down the problem number and move on. **If your software does not allow you to review problems, then guess and move on to Step 10.**

Step Seven — *Review skipped problems.*
While you are working problems, certain information may trigger an "Ah ha!" response. The "Ah ha!" response is when your brain suddenly remembers how to complete a problem. A memory from your homework or a lecture sometimes pops back into your head in the middle of a test. When this happens, immediately go back to the skipped problem and solve it. If you did not have an "Ah ha!" response while finishing other problems, go back and review the skipped problems and try to solve them anyway.

Step Eight — *Guess at the remaining problems.* If you cannot write down the first step, rewrite the problem. Also, remember that the way you learned how to solve a problem was by writing—not just looking at the problem. Sometimes, rewriting a problem jars your memory enough to complete the first step or the entire problem. Also, review your memory data dump to see if any of that information leads to writing the first step.

If you are taking a multiple choice test, take the answers and put them back into the equation to see which one is correct. Do the opposite of the process to see if you can work backwards to get the correct answer. For example, if you are asked to simplify $5(x + 2)$, then take the answer and do the opposite of the function to see if your answer is correct. The answer is $5x + 10$. The opposite of the function involves factoring $5x + 10$, which is $5(x + 2)$. This is the correct answer because it matches the problem you started with. Based on the time you are given, you may only solve a few problems using this strategy. However, even if you only solve a few problems you will still gain test points. If you still don't the answer to a problem, choose the middle range of potential answers. Often times, the correct answer is neither the highest nor lowest number listed in multiple choice fields. Whatever you do, always remember to select an answer for every problem.

Step Nine — *Review the test.* Review each problem by substituting the answer back into the equation or doing the opposite process required to answer the question. If you cannot check the problem in these ways, rework the problem on a separate sheet of paper and compare the answers. Look for careless errors or other errors you may have made. Students usually lose two to five test points on errors that could have been caught in review. Do not talk yourself out of an answer just because it was easy to solve.

Step Ten — *Use all of your alloted test time.* Do not close the test unless you have reviewed each problem twice, or, if you can't review problems, until you have finished all requirements. When working on the last problems, don't rush. This is an excellent time to make sure you get problems correct.

Even though we encourage students to use all of their test time, most don't. After talking to hundreds of these students, I have discovered two different themes for leaving the room early. First, test anxiety gets so overwhelming they cannot continue the test. The only way to lessen this anxiety is to finish before time is up—even though they may get a lower grade. Second, in computer-based settings, or in a testing center, students often rush through a test to avoid being the last to finish. They feel as though other students are watching and that those who finish last are "dumb and stupid." These students also believe students who hand their tests in first make "A's" and "B's," and those who finish last make "D's" and "F's." If you are one of these students, you don't need to care about what others think about you (it's usually wrong anyway).

Activity 5.5 Assessing Your Test-Review Methods

Before you can learn how to turn your old tests into handy study guides, you need to determine what you are currently doing with your tests and how well this method is working for you. Below, put a check by what you tend to do with your graded tests (you can mark more than one):

_____ Throw the test away

_____ Look at the grade and put the test in your book

_____ Review the test without working out missed problems

_____ Review the test and work out missed problems

_____ Compare the problems you missed with another student's problems

_____ Work problems that are similar to the ones that you missed

_____ Go over the missed problems with your tutor

_____ Go over the missed problems with your instructor

_____ Use the test review to develop new test-taking strategies

Other:

The Six Types of Test-Taking Errors

When students get their tests back they usually don't look at them. Some throw them away or stick them in their books and forget about them. In most cases it does not matter if the students make a good grade on the test or a poor grade. They do not like reviewing the tests. Some instructors make the students review the tests by going over them in class, but rarely do the students analyze the tests on their own. This leads to repeating mistakes. To assess your current test review methods, complete Activity 5.5 on the previous page.

As a comparison, imagine what would happen if your doctor gave you a blood test to see why you were sick, and you decided to just throw away the results and just pick some medicine off the shelf to see if it would cure you. The doctor would be sued for malpractice, and you may pick the wrong medicine and die. Perhaps the analogy exaggerates, but it makes the point. The real question is, "What do you do with your returned tests?"

Analyzing your math test will not kill you, but not doing it may kill your grades. Many students make the same mistakes over and over again, which causes them to fail too many tests. Students who analyze their tests are at a great advantage to determine how to improve on their next tests. These students find out the types of mistakes they made and now can change them. They develop better test-taking strategies for the next test and in most cases make higher scores. To improve future test scores, you must conduct a test analysis of previous tests.

In analyzing your tests, look for the following kinds of errors:
1. Misread-direction errors
2. Careless errors
3. Concept errors
4. Application errors
5. Test-taking errors
6. Study errors

Look at your last test to determine how many points you lost in the six types of test-taking errors. Analyze previous tests to determine if there is a pattern of errors. The type of errors is very important to determine how you can improve your studying and test-taking. For more information, visit the sample test printed at the back of this chapter.

Misread-Direction Errors

Now look at your last test. See how many points you lost to misread-direction errors. Misread-direction errors occur when you skip or misunderstand directions and do the problem incorrectly. If you do not understand if a problem you missed was a result of misread directions, ask the instructor for clarification.

Example 1: You have this type of problem to solve: (x + 1) (x + 1). Some students will try to solve for x, but the problem only calls for multiplication. You would solve for x only if you have an equation such as (x+1)(x+1) = 0.

Example 2: Another common mistake is not reading the directions before doing several word problems or statistical problems. All too often, when a test is returned, you find only three out of the five problems had to be completed. Even if you did get all five of them correct, it costs you valuable time, which could have been used obtaining additional test points.

To avoid misread-direction errors, carefully read and interpret all the directions. Look for anything that is unusual, or if the directions have two parts. If you do not understand the directions, ask the instructor for clarification. If you feel uneasy about asking the instructor for interpretation of the question, remember the instructor in most cases does not want to test you on the interpretation of the question but how you answer it. Also, you don't want to make the mistake of assuming that the instructor will not interpret the question. Let the instructor make the decision to interpret the question, not you.

Careless Errors

Careless errors are mistakes made because students lose complete focus on the question. If a student is nervous or in a hurry, little mistakes like switching signs mess up the entire problem. Sometimes, simple problems turn into nearly impossible problems if a student makes a careless error. This can really waste precious test time. Careless errors can be caught automatically when reviewing the test. Both good and poor math students make careless errors. Such errors can cost a student the difference of a letter grade on a test. Many students want all their errors to be careless errors when they analyze their

tests because it is easier to admit carelessness than admitting that they just didn't know the material. In such cases, I ask the student to solve the problem immediately while I watch. If the student can solve the problem or point out his/her mistake in a few seconds, it is a careless error. If the student cannot solve the problem immediately, it is not a careless error and is probably a concept error.

Careless Error Examples

1. Dropping the sign: -3(2x) = 6x, instead of -6x, which is the correct answer.
2. Not simplifying your answer: Leaving (3x -12)/3 as your answer instead of simplifying it to x - 4.
3. Adding fractions: 5/16 + 7/16 = 12/16 instead of 3/4.
4. Word problems: X = 15 instead of the "student had 15 tickets."

When working with students who make careless errors, I ask them two questions: First, "How many points did you lose due to careless errors?" Then I follow with, "How much time was left in the class period after you handed in your test?" Students who lose test points to careless errors are giving away points if they hand in their test papers before the test period ends. To reduce careless errors, you must realize the types of careless errors made and recognize them when reviewing your test. If you cannot solve the missed problem immediately, it is not a careless error. If your major error is not simplifying the answer, review each answer as if it were a new problem and try to reduce it.

Concept Errors

Concept errors are mistakes made when you do not understand the properties or principles required to work the problem. Concept errors, if not corrected, will follow you from test to test, causing you to lose a lot of points.

Some common concept errors are not knowing:

- $(-)(-)x = x$, not $-x$
- $-1(2) > x(-1)$ implies $2 < x$, not $2 > x$
- $5/0$ is undefined, not "0"
- $(a+x)/x$ is not simplified to "a"
- The order of operations
- $2 + 3 \times 5 = 17$, not 25
- $1/2 + 1/3 = 5/6$, not $2/5$

Concept errors must be corrected to improve your next math test score. Students who have numerous concept errors will fail the next test since each chapter builds on the previous ones. Just going back to rework the concept error problems is not good enough. You must go back to the textbook or notes and learn why you missed those types of problems, not just the one problem itself.

The best way to learn how to work those types of problems is to set up a concept-problem error page in the back of your notebook. Label the first page "Test One Concept errors." Write down all your concept errors and how to solve them. Then, work five more problems, which use the same concept. Now, in your own words, write the reasons that you can solve these problems.

If you cannot write the concept in your own words, you do not understand it. Get assistance from your instructor if you need help finding similar problems using the same concept or cannot understand the concept. Do this for every test. For example, when preparing for your second test, review the concept errors on the first test. Continue the process all the way into the final. This is a proven system to improve your test scores.

Application Errors

Application errors occur when you know the concept but cannot apply it to the problem. Application errors usually are found in word problems, deducing formulas (such as the quadratic equation) and graphing. Even some better students become frustrated

with application errors; they understand the material but cannot apply it to the problem.

To reduce application errors, you must predict the type of application problems that will be on the test, then think through and practice solving those types of problems using the concepts.

> Example: If you must derive the quadratic formula, you should practice doing that backward and forward while telling yourself the concept used to move from one step to the next.

Application errors are common with word problems. When solving word problems, look for the key phrases displayed in the "Translating English Words into Algebraic Expressions" figure to help you set up the problem. After completing the word problem, reread the question to make sure you have applied the answer to the intended question.

Application errors can be avoided with appropriate practice and insight. However, if all else fails, memorize a word problem or a graphing problem and use it as part of your memory data dump. Write it down on your test and use it as an example to solve the problems on the test.

Test-Taking Errors

Test-taking errors apply to the specific way you take tests. Some students consistently make the same types of test-taking errors. Through recognition, these bad test-taking habits can be replaced by good test-taking habits. The result will be higher test scores. The list that follows includes the test-taking errors, which can cause you to lose many points on an exam.

Error 1— *Missing more questions in the first third, second third or last third part of a test.* Divide your test in thirds. For example, if your test had 20 problems, look at the number of points missed from problems 1 through 6. How many points were missed from problems 7 through 13? How many points were missed from problems 14 to 20? Missing more questions in the first third of a test could be caused by carelessness when doing easy problems or from test anxiety. Missing questions in the last part of the test could be due to the fact that the last problems are more difficult than the earlier questions or due to increasing your test speed to finish the test.

If you consistently miss more questions in a certain part of the test, use your remaining test time to review that section of the test first. This means you may review the last part of your test first.

Error 2— *Not completing a problem to its last step.* If you have this bad habit, review the last step of the test problem first before doing an in-depth test review.

Error 3— *Changing correct answers to incorrect answers.* Look for erased answers on your test. I have seen students erase the correct way to solve the problem, and thus the correct answer, and then change it to an incorrect answer. I have asked these students why they erased the correct answer. In almost every case the student said that the answer was too easy to solve, so they thought it was wrong. These students need to build their test-taking confidence and know how to check their answers. If this is you, make sure you learn how to check your answers and have confidence in them.

On multiple choice tests, most students indicate that they are bad answer changers. That is because they only remember changing answers from right to wrong. They usually do not remember the times they change answers from wrong to right.

Now, let's see if you are a good, bad or neutral answer changer. On multiple choice problems, you can change your answer three ways: from right to wrong, wrong to right and wrong to wrong. Look at the eraser marks on your answer sheet that represent the number of answers that you changed. You may want

to do this on several of your tests. Count the number of changes that represent the three categories and change them into percents.

If you have a pattern of changing over 50 percent of your answers from wrong to right then keep changing your answers. If over 50 percent of your answers are changed from right to wrong then stop changing answers. If the three categories of changing answers are about the same, then do what makes you feel the best because it is not affecting your grade.

If you don't have previous tests to measure the effectiveness of your answer changing, then wait to review several tests before you make your decision. If you are indeed a bad answer changer, then on test day use a pencil without an eraser to mark your multiple choice tests. This should stop you from changing your answers.

Error 4— *Getting stuck on one problem and spending too much time on it.* You need to set a time limit on each problem before moving to the next problem. Working too long on a problem without success will increase your test anxiety and waste valuable time that could be used in solving other problems or in reviewing your test. For example, if your test has twenty problems that must be completed in one hour, how long should you spend on each problem? You should spend a maximum of three minutes on each problem depending on the complexity of the problems. Spending more than three minutes, unless it is the last problem you are working on, can cost you test points.

Error 5— *Rushing through the easiest part of the test and making careless errors.* This happens even to the best students. If you have the bad habit of getting more points taken off for the easy problems than for the hard problems, first review the easy problems and then the hard ones.

Error 6— *Incorrectly copying an answer from your scratch paper to your test.* To avoid these kinds of errors, systematically compare your last problem step on scratch paper with the answer written on the test. In addition, always hand in your scratch work with your test.

Error 7— *Leaving answers blank.* If you look at a problem and cannot figure out how to solve it, do not leave it blank. Write down some information about the problem, rewrite the problem or try to do at least the first step.

Error 8— *Answering only the first step in a two-step problem.* These students get so excited when answering the first step of the problem that they forget about the second step. This is especially true on two-step word problems. To correct this test-taking error, write "two" in the margin of the problem. That will remind you that there are two steps or two answers to this problem.

Error 9— *Not understanding all of the functions of your calculator.* Some students barely learn how to use critical calculator functions. Then they forget or have to relearn how to use calculators during a test, which costs test points and time. Do not wait to learn how to use your calculator on the test. Over-learn the use of your calculator *before* the test.

Error 10— *Completing the test early without checking all of your answers.* Do not worry about the first person who finishes the test and leaves. Many students get nervous when other students start to leave early. This can lead to test anxiety, mental blocks and loss of recall. According to research, the first students to finish a test do not always get the best grades. It sometimes is the exact opposite. Ignore those students who leave and use the full time allowed.

Error 11— *Trying to complete problems in your head.* This is especially common among distance learners and students in Emporium model courses. These student get into this habit while doing online homework. Doing problems in your head causes you to lose points. Make sure to write down your steps so that you are able to check your work.

Error 12— *When taking a timed test on a computer, many students do not use the last few minutes effectively.* If students cannot review their test answers, they do not slow down and check all the last questions to make sure the problems are correct. If they can check their answers, then they do not go back and do it because they think it is a waste of time. Both types of students are wasting time and losing test points.

Study Errors

Study errors, the last type of mistake to look for in a test analysis, occur when you study the wrong type of material or do not spend enough time on pertinent material. Review your test to find out if you missed problems because you did not practice that type of problem or because you did practice it but forgot how to do it during the test. Study errors will take some time to track down, but correcting them helps you on future tests.

   Most students, after analyzing one or several tests, will recognize at least one major, common test-taking error. Understanding the effects of this error should change your study techniques or test-taking strategy.

Example: If there are seven minutes left in the test, should you review for careless errors or try to answer those two problems you could not totally solve? This is a trick question. The real question is, "Do you miss more points due to careless errors or concept errors, or are the missed points about even?" The answer to this question should determine how you will spend the last minutes of the test. If you missed more points due to careless errors or missed about the same number of points due to careless/concept errors, review for careless errors.

How to Prepare for a Final Exam

The first day of class is when you start preparing for the final exam. Look at the syllabus or ask the instructor if the final exam is cumulative. A cumulative exam covers everything from the first chapter to the last chapter. Most math final exams are cumulative. The second question you should ask is if the final exam is a departmental exam or if your instructor makes it up. In most cases, departmental exams are more difficult and need a little different preparation. If you have a departmental final, you need to ask for last year's test and ask other students what their instructors say will be on the test.

The third question is, how much will the final exam count? Does it carry the same weight as a regular test or, as in some cases, will it count for a third of your grade? If the latter is true, the final exam will usually make a letter grade difference on your final course grade. The final exam could also determine if you pass or fail the course. Knowing this information before the final exam will help you prepare. You also need to calculate the numerical grade you need to make on the final to pass your course with the grade you want. Knowing this before the exam will help decide how much study time you need.

The fourth question is, do students have to pass the final exam to pass the course. Some math departments set up final exams as an exit exam to the next course. They know that the final exam is an accumulation of all the course knowledge and predicts success in the next course. Knowing all this information before taking the finial will help you prepare.

Preparing for the final exam is similar to preparing for each chapter test. You must create a pretest to discover what you have forgotten. You can use questions from the textbook chapter tests or questions from your study group. Review the concept errors that you recorded in the back of your notebook labeled "Test One," "Test Two," etc. Review your problem log for questions you consistently miss. Even review material that you knew for the first and second test but which was not used on any other tests. Students forget how to work some of these problems.

If you do not have a concept error page for each chapter and did not keep a problems log you need to develop a pre-test before taking the final exam. If you are individually preparing for the final, then copy each chapter test and do every fourth problem to see what errors you may make. However, it is better to have a study group where each of the four members brings in ten problems with the answers worked out on a separate page. Then each group member can take the 30-question test to find out what they need to study. You can refer to the answers to help you solve the problems that you miss. For an example of how to analyze a previous test, review the boxes printed on the next page.

Math Test for Prealgebra

The answers are in boldface. The correct answers to missed questions are shaded. Identify the type of error based on the Six Types of Test-Taking Errors. The student's test score is 70. The answer key is on the next page.

1. Write in words: 32.685

   Thirty-two and six hundred eighty-five thousanths

2. Write as a fraction and simplify: 0.078

   $\dfrac{78}{1000}$ $\boxed{\dfrac{39}{500}}$

3. Round to the nearest hundredth: 64.8653

   64.865 $\boxed{64.87}$ *-4*

4. Combine like terms: 6.78x - 3.21 + 7.23x - 6.19

   = 6.78x + 7.23x + (-3.21) + (-6.19)
   = 14.01x - 9.4

5. Divide and round to the nearest hundredth: 68.1357÷2.1

   32.4454 ➜ 32.45

6. Write as a decimal: $\dfrac{5}{16}$

   0.3125

7. Insert < or > to make a true statement.

   $\dfrac{3}{8}$ **<** $\dfrac{6}{13}$

8. Solve: $\dfrac{3}{x} = \dfrac{9}{12}$ *-2*

   9x = 3(12)

   $\dfrac{x}{9} = \dfrac{36}{9}$

   x = 5 $\boxed{x = 4}$

9. What number is 35% of 60?   *-4*

   2100 $\boxed{21.00}$

10. 20.8 is 40% of what number?   *-8*

    $\boxed{52}$

11. 567 is what percent of 756?   *-8*

    $\dfrac{756}{567} = \dfrac{9}{100}$

    = 133.3% $\boxed{75\%}$

12. Multiply: *-2*

    (-6.03) (-2.31) = 13.9 $\boxed{13.9293}$

Answer Key for Prealgebra Test

1. Correct
2. *Misread-directions error*—forgot to simplify by reducing the fraction.
3. *Concept error*—did not know that hundredths is two places to the right of the decimal.
4. Correct
5. Correct
6. Correct
7. Correct
8. *Careless error*—divided incorrectly in the last step.
9. *Test-taking error*—did not follow step 5 in test-taking steps: reviewing answers to see if they make sense. The number that equals 35% of 60 can't be larger than 60.
10. *Test-taking error*—did not follow steps 7 and 8 in test-taking steps: don't leave an answer blank.
11. *Application error*—solved the equation correctly but the equation setup was wrong.
12. *Concept error*—did not know that when you multiply with one number in the hundredths, the answer must include the hundredths column.

Chapter Five: Checklist for Knowledge and Behaviors

Put a check after understanding the knowledge statements and fill in the behavioral activities.

Chapter Knowledge

1. I understand that math anxiety affects learning in class and doing homework _____

2. I know that test anxiety is a learned behavior developed by having emotional and/or worry response during previous tests._____

3. I know that some test anxiety can improve performance; however too much test anxiety can decrease performance._____

4. I understand the two types of text anxiety (emotional, worry) and how they can affect me in different ways._____

5. I know that test anxiety reduces my ability to complete tests, because it blocks memory and causes an urgency to leave the room before checking all my answers._____

6. I know that I must learn relaxation techniques to help reduce my anxiety._____

7. I understand that just completing homework and attending class does not guarantee that I will pass my math tests._____

8. I understand that I should not cram for math tests. _____

9. I know to follow the 10 Steps to Taking a Math Test to obtain the greatest number of points in the least amount of time. _____

10. I know that students who turn their test in first or last make "A's" and "B's". _____

11. I know that without conducting a test analysis, I will probably continue to make the same old test errors and lose valuable test points. _____

12. I know to review my Concept Errors from each previous test before the next test. _____

Behavioral Activities

1. I have selected my two best short-term relaxation techniques and will practice them three times a week. _____

2. I will manage my self-talk about math by reducing my negative statements and changing them to positive statements._____

3. I have developed my own memory data dump for my next test and have practiced writing down the information. _____

4. I developed my own steps to taking a math test. _____

5. I review each test using the Six Types of Test-taking Errors. _____

Name: _____   Date: _____

Assignment for Chapter 5

1. List and explain three causes of math anxiety. Which cause would you most likely have?

2. List and describe three ways to help overcome math anxiety.

3. List and describe five causes of test anxiety.

4. Describe your best short-term relaxation technique.

5. List three positive statements you can tell yourself during the test.

6. List four reasons for why you can understand how to do the math problems in class but can still miss them on the test.

7. List four reasons how you can correctly complete all the homework assignments and still not score highly on math tests.

8. List and describe the Ten Steps for Better Test-Taking (either online or in-class).

9. List and describe the Six Types of Test-Taking errors:

10. Complete a test analysis on your last test. List two types of errors you made and how you can correct them.

ASSESSING AND USING YOUR MEMORY AND MATH LEARNING STRATEGIES

6

IN CHAPTER 6
YOU WILL LEARN THESE CONCEPTS:

✓ How a student's affective characteristics influence success

✓ How understanding the Stages of Memory improves learning

✓ How to determine an use your best learning preference

✓ General memory techniques

✓ How to develop "My Math Success Plan"

Ingredients for Math Success

Now that you have learned about study skills, we need to look at the ingredients for success and understand the variables that affect your math success. Before we start exploring your learning skills, however, it helps to understand the keys to academic success. Dr. Benjamin Bloom, a famous researcher of educational learning, discovered that IQ (intelligence) and "cognitive entry skills" (knowledge about math) account for 50 percent of a student's course grade. This is highlighted in the Bloom Chart, printed on the next page. As you can see, quality of instruction represents 25 percent of a course grade, while "affective student characteristics" reflect the remaining 25 percent. New research suggests affective characteristics account for 41 percent of academic achievment, leaving 34 percent for entry skills (Zientek, et. 2013). Dr. Bloom's four variables to academic achievement are as follows:

- *Intelligence* is how fast a person can learn or relearn math concepts of varying difficulty.

- *Cognitive entry skills* refer to how much math people already know before entering a math course.

- *Quality of instruction* concerns the effectiveness of math instructors, lab assistants and tutors when presenting material to students in the classroom, math lab and while tutoring. This effectiveness depends on the course textbooks, curriculum, teaching style, tutoring style, and teaching aids.

- *Affective student characteristics* are characteristics people possess which affect their course grades, excluding how much math they knew before entering a math course. These affective characteristics include anxiety, study skills, study attitudes, self-concepts, motivation and test-taking skills.

What You Know About Math Affects Your Grades

Going into a class with poor math knowledge sets you up for achieving low grades. A student placed in a math course that requires a more extensive math background than he or she possesses will probably fail that course. Without the correct math background, you may fall behind and never catch up. The following information is important to know in order to make sure that you are placed in the proper math course.

The math you need to know to enroll in a particular math course can be measured by a placement test. Most colleges and universities use a standardized test such as the ACT, SAT, or Accuplacer to place students into math courses. However, some institutions use their own tests to place students. It is important to remember that the grades you earned in prerequisite math courses measure your level of math knowledge. However, a few students are still incorrectly placed in math courses by these resources. So, it is important to talk to your advisor and instructor to provide any other information that might assist in properly placing you into a math course.

How Quality of Instruction Affects Your Grades

Quality of instruction accounts for another 25 percent of your grade (or possibly less in computer-based courses). This includes classroom atmosphere, the instructor's teaching style, lab instruction, textbook content, and format. All of these factors affect the ability to learn in the classroom.

Interestingly, probably the most important "quality" variable is the compatibility of an instructor's teaching style with the students'. First, you need to discover your learning preference. Second, try to find an instructor who best matches this preference. Sometimes this is difficult to find out, but a good place to start is to talk to the chair of the math department. The department chair knows the faculty. Advisors, too, know the teaching styles of every member of a math faculty. The key is to start your inquiry early enough to get into the class that bests suits your needs.

If you cannot find an instructor to match your learning preference, improving math study skills and using a math lab or learning resource center can compensate for this. You and your instructor might not be the best match, but it is still your responsibility to be successful in the course.

Math departments design courses so that each course covers certain math concepts. Ideally, each course curriculum prepares students for the next level of math. However, sometimes the courses have gaps between them, or an instructor doesn't cover all the material required, leaving students unprepared for their next courses. If this happens, go to your instructor immediately to explain that you did not cover the math in your previous course. Your instructor will suggest a way for you to learn it.

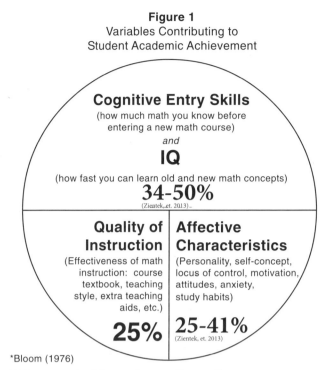

Figure 1
Variables Contributing to
Student Academic Achievement

Cognitive Entry Skills
(how much math you know before entering a new math course)
and
IQ
(how fast you can learn old and new math concepts)
34-50%
(Zientek, et. 2013)

Quality of Instruction
(Effectiveness of math instruction: course textbook, teaching style, extra teaching aids, etc.)
25%

Affective Characteristics
(Personality, self-concept, locus of control, motivation, attitudes, anxiety, study habits)
25-41%
(Zientek, et. 2013)

*Bloom (1976)

How Affective Student Characteristics Influence Your Grades

Affective student characteristics account for about 25-41 percent of your grade. These affective characteristics include math study skills, test anxiety, motivation, locus of control, learning preference, and other variables that determine your ability to learn math.

Most students do not have this 25 to 41 percent of their grade working in their favor. In fact, most students have never been taught any study skills at all, let alone math-specific study skills. It is also true that many students do not know their learning preferences, which means they may study ineffectively by using those that are least effective. Until recently, little attention has been devoted to how students learn, so it is not unusual if you do not know what your learning preferences are. Later in this chapter you will have the opportunity to explore the ways you learn most effectively.

Boylan (2011) also interviewed Dr. Nolting concluding that improving student affective learning is the fastest way to improve math success.

Understanding the Stages of Memory

Now that you understand the ingredients for math success, we need to review the learning process to determine your learning strengths and areas for improvement. To do this, you must first understand how memory works. You learn by conditioning and thinking, but memorization is different from learning. For memorization, the brain must perform several tasks including receiving, storing and recalling information. By understanding how memory works, you learn at which point your memory fails you. Most students experience memory trouble between the time the brain receives information and the time the information is stored. There are many learning techniques that can help you receive and store information without losing it.

How You Learn

Educators tell us that learning is the process of "achieving competency." Simply put, it is how you become good at something. The three ways of learning are by conditioning, thinking and a combination of conditioning and thinking. *Conditioning* is learning things with a maximum of physical and emotional reaction and a minimum of thinking. *Thinking* is defined as learning with a maximum of thought and a minimum of emotional and physical reaction.

Conditioning Example: Repeating the word "pi" to yourself and practicing where the symbol is found on a calculator are two forms of conditioned learning. This type of learning involves the use of your voice and hand-eye coordination, both of which require very little thinking.

Thinking Example: Learning about "pi" by thinking is different than learning about it by conditioning. To learn "pi" by thinking, you would have to do the calculations necessary to result in the numeric value, which the word "pi" represents. You are learning, using your mind (thought activities), and you are using very little emotional or physical energy to learn "pi" in this way.

Years of research indicates that the best way to learn math is to combine conditioning with thinking. The most successful way to do this is to learn by thinking first and conditioning second.

Learning by thinking means you learn by:

- Observing,

- Processing and

- Understanding the information.

The Stages of Memory

Sensory Input
Hearing, Seeing, Feeling,
Smelling, Tasting
Impaired Senses

Chart Guide: On this chart, the stages of memory are listed in orange ovals. Inside, you'll find each stage's function, as well as problems that occur when it is impaired. Above the dotted lines, you'll find the exact type of "forgetting" that occurs when these impairments affect you memory.

Sensory Register
Determining Important
Information to Learned
Poor Note-Taking Cues

Forgetting
Information Not Processed

Short-Term Memory
Keeping Information in
Mind to Take Notes
*Poor Memory or
Note-Taking Skills*

Forgetting
Information Not Rehearsed

Working Memory
Rehearsing Information by
Studying/Homework
*Not Enough Practice/Effective
Fluency of Information*

Forgetting
Information Not Understood

Abstract Reasoning
Understanding Math
Concepts
Not Generalized

Forgetting
*Information Not
Reviewed*

Long-Term Memory
Knowledge of Facts
Poor or No Recall of Facts

Forgetting
Information Not Reviewed

Memory Output
Written or Verbal
Test-Taking Skills
*Anxiety/Lack of Knowledge
or Concepts*

Understanding the Stages of Memory

Memory is different from learning; it requires the reception, storage and retrieval of information. This memory process was mentioned in previous chapters and will now be discussed in detail. The memory process starts with the sensory input, proceeds through the sensory register into short-term memory, and then into working memory, where it goes directly into long-term memory, abstract reasoning or memory output (see the Stages of Memory chart).

Information also goes through long-term memory and/or abstract reasoning and then into memory output. The double arrows in the Stages of Memory Chart demonstrate how working memory goes both ways. The reception of information is through the sensory input. The storage is through the sensory register, short-term memory, working memory, long-term memory and abstract reasoning. The retrieval of this information is usually through doing homework and taking tests. It is important to understand that information can be lost through each stage.

As we discuss each stage of memory, locate your memory strengths and where your memory is breaking down. Understanding how the stages of memory affect learning helps improve your grades.

Sensory Input and Sensory Register

You receive information through your five senses (known as the sensory input): what you see, feel, hear, smell and taste. This process behaves differently in every course.

The sensory register briefly holds an exact image or sound of each sensory experience until it can be processed. If the information is not processed immediately, it is forgotten. The sensory register helps us go from one situation to the next without cluttering up our minds with trivial information. Processing the information involves placing it into short-term memory. Students who don't attend class do not ever reach this stage of memory and lose valuable information. This stage is also affected by attention in the classroom. If you are not paying attention or are distracted, then information is not being inputted into your memory system.

If students have visual or auditory impairments, information must be processed differently or through another sense. For example, deaf students may need interpreters or real time captioning while visually impaired students may need large print, audiobooks, recorded lectures or Braille texts.

The sensory register is also the memory stage in which students determine if information is important or if they can discard it. Students need to use note-taking cues to write down important information instead of writing *everything* down, which can leads to a lack of concentration and learning.

> Example: In math classes, you use your sense of vision to watch the instructor demonstrate problems and to read printed materials. You use your sense of hearing to listen to the instructor and other students discuss problems. Your sense of touch is used to operate your calculator and to appreciate geometric shapes. In chemistry and other classes, however, you may additionally use your senses of smell and taste to identify substances.

How Short-Term Memory Affects What You Remember

Information that passes through the sensory register is stored in short-term memory. Short-term memory involves visual information or auditory information. Remembering something for a short time is not hard for most students. By conscious effort, you remember the math laws, facts and formulas received by your five senses. You recognize and register them in your mind as something to remember for a short time.

Psychologists have found that short-term

memory cannot hold an unlimited amount of information. You may be able to use short-term memory to remember a person's name or a few formulas, but items placed into short-term memory usually fade fast, as the name suggests.

Example: When you are studying math, you can tell yourself the distributive property is illustrated by $a(b+c)=ab+ac$. By deliberately telling yourself to remember that fact (by using conditioning — repeating or writing it again and again), you can remember it, at least for a while, because you have put it in short-term memory.

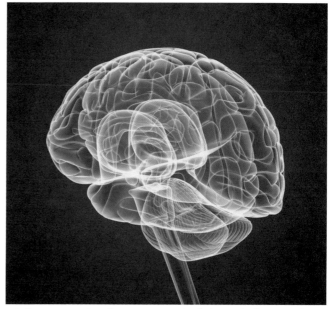

In many college classes, information is processed so quickly that no time is allowed for practicing and understanding the math. Instructors are required to cover an immense amount of information and students are lucky if they capture all of it and understand it for a brief moment. The memory process, for the most part, stops at short term in the classroom. That's why students need to have good note-taking skills to record the information as effectively as possible, so it can be reviewed later on for better understanding.

Example: Looking up an email address in the school registry, then forgetting it before you can type it. Learning the name of a person at a large party or in a class but forgetting it completely within a few seconds. Cramming for a test and forgetting most of it before taking the test.

How Working Memory Affects What You Remember

Working memory (or long-term retrieval) is that process in the brain that works on problems for a longer period of time than short-term memory. Working memory, then, offers an increase in the amount of time information is held in memory. (An increase in the volume of information that can be held requires long-term memory.)

Working memory is like the amount of RAM in a computer. Working memory uses the information (such as multiplication tables) recalled from long-term memory, along with new information to learn new concepts. It is the ability to think about and use many pieces of information at the same time. For instance, when you solve a linear equation in a math class you must use all the math that you learned in elementary school like addition, subtraction, and multiplication. You then have to add this to the new rules for linear equations.

Working memory can be compared to a mental workspace or an internal chalkboard. Just like a chalkboard, working memory has limited space, which can cause a "bottleneck" in learning. It involves the ability to recall information after learning has been consistently interrupted over a period of several minutes. Students with working memory problems may listen to a lecture and understand the information as it is explained. When the instructor goes back to something discussed earlier, however, the student has difficulty explaining or remembering things they thought they knew just a few minutes earlier. These students have difficulty remembering series of steps long enough to understand the concept.

Students also use working memory to do their homework. This is why students avoid or don't understand homework have problems learning: they don't practice enough to learn concepts. Studying every night also helps put information into long term memory which makes it easier when it is time to use working memory to learn new information.

Working memory goes both ways in the memory process. First, it leads into long-term memory and abstract reasoning. Second, it brings information out from long-term memory and abstract memory to use in learning new concepts. How information is remembered largely depends upon the subject. When learning a mathematical concept, working memory goes into abstract memory. When learning historical dates or definitions of words, information goes directly into long-term memory. Students use working memory to do their homework and when answering test questions. The amount of space in working memory is critical to answering test questions just like the amount of RAM is critical to running computer programs.

Research indicates test anxiety affects

Example: In calculating 26 x 32, you would put the intermediate products 52 (from 2 x 26) and 780 (from 30 x 26 — remember 3 is in the 10's place, so make it 30) into working memory and add them together. The more automatic the multiplication, the less working memory you use. If you cannot remember your multiplication, you use up working memory trying to solve the multiplication problem.

working memory. Many students who have test anxiety indicate that during tests they recognize problems but cannot remember how to work them. This happens because anxiety takes up working memory space, leaving less to solve problems. When anxiety levels decrease, such as right after a test, students remember how to solve problems as their working memory is freed up. This accounts for the "I knew I knew it" syndrome.

How Long-Term Memory Affects What You Remember

Long-term memory is a storehouse of material that is retained for long periods of time. Working memory places information in long-term memory and long-term memory is recalled into working memory to solve problems. It is not a matter of trying harder to remember unrelated facts or ideas; it is a matter of organizing your short-term memories and working memories into meaningful information.

In most cases long-term memory is immeasurable. There is so much room in long-term memory, no one has measured its total capacity. Long-term memory also relates more to language skills than abstract skills. Students with good long-term memory and poor abstract skills can sometimes do well in every subject except math and the physical sciences. These students can use their long-term memory language skills by learning the vocabulary. By understanding the language of mathematics they can put into words how to solve math problems and recall these words during the test instead of depending mainly on their abstract memory. This information must be reviewed many times to get into longterm memory, then again to *keep* it there.

How Reasoning Affects What You Remember

Reasoning (abstract memory) is thinking about memories, comprehending their meanings and understanding their concepts. Abstract reasoning involves learning how the rules and laws apply to solving math problems. Without understanding a concept, you cannot transfer information into abstract reasoning.

The main problem most students face is converting information from working memory to long-term and abstract reasoning. To place information into long-term memory, students must understand math vocabulary and practice problems. To place information into abstract reasoning, students must understand a concept and remember it. Most students use long-term memory and abstract reasoning to solve problems. However, without abstract reasoning, they have difficulty generalizing concepts.

Role of Memory Output in Testing

Memory output is what educators call a "retrieving process." It is necessary for verbal or written examinations. The retrieving process is used when answering questions, doing homework or taking tests. It is the method by which you recall information stored into long-term memory and, through abstract reasoning, verbalize it or put it on paper.

This retrieval process comes directly from long-term memory. For example, "What are whole numbers?" This is a fact question that comes from long-term memory. The retrieval process also comes from abstract reasoning. However, most math problems are solved through working memory by using information from both long-term memory and abstract reasoning. For example, "solve: 3y -10 = 9y + 21". For this problem you are pulling in number facts from long-term memory and the rules for solving equations from abstract reasoning.

Three things block memory output: insufficient processing of information into long-term memory or reasoning, test anxiety, and poor test-taking skills. If you do not place all of the information you learned into long-term memory and abstract reasoning, you may not be able to answer test questions. Test anxiety decreases your ability to recall important information or totally blocks information. During exams it affects memory output by decreasing working memory speed and how much information it processes at one time. Students who work on decreasing anxiety and improving test-taking skills often improve their memory output.

Student Scenarios

Before we start assessing your memory strengths and areas to improve let's look at some students that may be in similar situations. Read the following scenarios and decide the area that needs to be improved, as well as possible strengths. There could be more than one successful stage.

Scenario #1: Jack

Jack is a student who was successful in high school math courses but is having difficulty in his Intermediate Algebra course. He remembers his high school math well enough; however, his college instructor moves much faster than he's used to. Still, during lectures, he decides to check his social media feeds on his phone (just as he had in high school). By the time Jack looks up, he doesn't know what the problem is, let alone how to solve it. He tells himself that he'll just figure it out later and soon gets distracted when a classmate texts him about a date he'd gone on the night before. What is Jack's previous stage strength? What stage is blocking his learning? What can he do about it?

Scenario #2: Sally

Sally has been out of high school for several years. She's in Elementary Algebra in her first semester and has failed her first test. She does her homework, but she has problems reviewing notes before a test. Her instructor says that understanding his lectures is the key to success. When taking notes, she either writes everything down or almost nothing. When asked about her note-taking, she says that she starts to write everything down, gets behind, and gives up. What is Sally's successful stage? What stage blocks her learning? What can she do about it?

Scenario #3: Bill

Bill just graduated from high school and is in College Algebra. He's a business major. He pays attention in class but made a D on his first test. While in the Learning Support Center, a tutor asks to see his notes. His notes are sketchy, missing several steps for problems. Bill says he knows what to write down and does his homework. However, the instructor says that many of test questions come from lecture concepts. What is Bill's successful stage? What stage blocks his learning? What can he do about it?

Scenario #4: Penny

Penny is a returning working parent and is in Intermediate Algebra for the second time. She makes a low C on her first test without studying much because most of it is review. Her instructor says students who make a C or lower on the first test have difficulty passing the course. She understands information in class; however, she cannot remember how to do some test problems. Due to her work schedule, she has difficulty studying and doing homework. Sometimes she rushes through just to get it done. She's afraid she may not pass the course again. What is Penny's successful stage? What blocks her learning? What can she do about it?

Scenario #5: Jose

Jose is in an Elementary Algebra course after working for five years. He wants to get a good degree to be eligible for a promotion. He attends night courses, pays attention, and does all his homework. In fact, he gets A's on his homework, but makes a C on his first test. His employer says she will pay for his future courses if he makes a B average or higher. However, since he has high homework scores, Jose does not take notes from online problems or review much before the test. He is worried that he will not make a B in the class. What is Jose's successful stage? What stage is blocking his learning? What can he do about it?

Scenario #6: Wynn

Wynn is in Elementary Algebra for the second time and has a 3.50 GPA. He is a good student majoring in Sociology. His other courses come easy, but math troubles him. He studies math about 15 hours a week and reviews before each test; however, he does not pass his first test. He memorizes problems and formulas, but has difficulty solving problems on the tests because they are different than the homework. He only needs math and a few other courses to get his A.A. degree. What is Wynn's successful stage? What stage blocks his learning? What can he do about it?

Scenario #7: Fitz

Fitz is in Calculus I for the first time. He has made good grades in his previous math courses. He's an engineering major and needs to make A's and B's in his Calculus courses to be accepted into a graduate engineering program. During his first test, he feels sick and his heart races. Though he understands the concepts, these symptoms cause him to lose focus. Afterward, he feels better. In fact, he remembers how to do the problems he missed. Still, for the first time in his life, he makes a D on a math test. Now he's afraid that he won't pass Calculus and he's going to have to change majors. What is Fitz's successful stage? What stage blocks his memory? What can he do about it?

Scenario Answers

Scenario #1: Jack. What is Jack's previous stage strength? Long-term Memory. He remembers his high school math. What stage blocks his learning? Sensory Input. Distractions cause him to miss information. What can he do about it? Sit closer to his instructor and stop looking at his phone.

Scenario #2: Sally. What is Sally's previous stage strength? Working Memory. She does her homework. What stage blocks her learning? Sensory Register. She does not know what is important to write down, so she writes down everything. This leads to her not understanding lectures, so she does not have notes to review for tests. What can she do about it? She needs to learn note-taking cues. That way she can pay more attention and have better notes to review.

Scenario #3: Bill. What are Bill's previous stage strengths? Sensory Input, Sensory Register, and Working Memory. He pays attention in class, knows what to write down, and does his homework. What stage blocks his learning? Short-Term Memory. He does not have the memory to take notes and/or does not have a note system. What can he do about it? Use a note-taking system and, with permission from his instructor, record the class and take pictures of difficult problems.

Scenario #4: Penny. What are Penny's stage strengths? Short-Term Memory and probably most previous stages. She knows information in class. What stage blocks her learning? Working Memory. She doesn't complete her homework. Without practice, information can't go into Long-Term Memory or Abstract Reasoning. What can she do about it? Complete and understand her homework, then practice more through tutoring.

Scenario #5: Jose. What are Jose's previous stage strengths? Sensory Register and Working Memory. He pays attention and does his homework. What stage blocks learning? Long-Term Memory and maybe Short-Term Memory. He does not take notes from his homework, which means there is little to review. He does not review material before a test, and the review process places information into Long-term Memory. What can he do about it? Take notes from his homework and review material before a test.

Scenario #6: Wynn. What are Wynn's previous stage strengths? Working and Long-Term Memory. He studies math 15 hours a week, knows the formulas, and reviews before each test. What stage blocks learning? Abstract Reasoning. He spends enough time learning math; however, despite his good grades in other classes, he has a hard time understanding mathematical concepts. What can he do about it? He needs to meet with his instructor and talk about his math learning problem. He may need to use manipulatives, as well as math-specific study skills. He also needs to talk with a math lab supervisor and ask about taking a liberal arts or statistics course that involves less abstract reasoning.

Scenario #7: Fitz. What are Fitz's previous stage strengths? Abstract Reasoning. He understands the concepts. What stage blocks learning? Memory Output and maybe Working Memory. He understands the concepts; however, he seems to deal with test anxiety. This anxiety blocks memory output and reduces working memory. What can he do about it? He needs to learn relaxation techniques and visit a counselor. Also, he needs to develop a test-taking plan.

Now that you've analyzed these students' strengths and areas of improvement in the stages of memory, it's time for you to assess

your own. You may have more than one strength and more than one area you need to improve on. Afterward, you can use this information to improve your learning and/or show your knowledge on tests.

Assessing Your Memory Strengths and Weaknesses

Understanding the stages of memory helps answer this common question about learning math: "Why do I understand the procedures to solve a problem one day and forget how to solve a similar problem days later?"

First, after initially learning how to solve the problem, you did not rehearse the solving process enough for it to enter your long-term memory. Second, you got the information into long-term memory, but did not review it frequently enough. Third, you memorized how to work the problem but did not understand the concept. There are also other areas where the memory process breaks down. The following are common problems students have in learning, preceded by what stages of memory each problem affects:

Sensory Input
- Visual or hearing impairment.
- Dyslexia.
- Not paying attention

Sensory Register
- Trouble understanding information in a noisy classroom.
- Not discerning important information.

Short-Term Memory
- Being a poor note-taker.
- Can't write down problem steps.

Working Memory
- Having a poor homework system.
- Not reading the text.
- Not doing or completing homework
- Procrastinating

Long-Term Memory
- Not reviewing homework problems or notes.
- Not knowing vocabulary.

Abstract Reasoning
- Not understanding or applying properties, rules, and key concepts.

Memory Output
- Breakdown in one or more stages of memory.
- Inadequate test-taking skills.
- Test anxiety.

Activity 6.1 Discovering Your Memory Strengths

Now that you have a better understanding of the stages of memory, it is time to do a self-assessment to discover your memory strengths and those areas in which you need to improve. Look at the Stages of Memory Chart and put an "S" by those memory stages in which you are strong. Label your average memory stages with an "A." Put a "W" by those areas you consider yourself weak. Once you have done this, answer the questions printed below.

1. What weak area(s) did you have in the Stages of Memory and how can you improve them?

2. In what area(s) are you average, according to the Stages of Memory, and how can you improve them?

3. What were your strong areas in the Stages of Memory about which you can be proud?

Determining Your Best Learning Preference

A learning preference is a description of the cognitive, affective, and physiological factors that shape the way a student inputs material to be learned and then demonstrates the knowledge of the material. Learning preferences also pertain to the best time of day to study, environmental factors (silence, music, lights) and how the brain best processes the material. Research has shown that students who understand learning preferences improve learning effectiveness in and outside of the classroom. Many inventories are available, and students should talk to their instructors or counselors about taking one or more.

There are different types of learning preference assessments. One type focuses on learning modalities while other assessments focus on cognitive or environmental learning preferences. In this chapter we will focus on modality learning preferences.

Learning Modalities (Using Your Senses)

Learning modalities focus on the best way your brain receives information; that is, learning *visually* (seeing), *auditorially* (hearing) or *kinesthetically* (touching, hands-on). If one is available, take a learning preference inventory that measures learning modalities. Even better, take an inventory that measures learning modalities specifically for math, such as the Learning Modality Inventory for Math Students (Nolting, 2008). Other learning-preference inventories measure learning preferences, but they mainly focus on English or reading-learning modes. Sometimes students have different learning preferences for math, so an inventory that measures

subject-specific learning preferences is ideal. Take the Learning Modality Inventory for Math Students, found in Appendix B, to better understand your prefered way to learn math. Based on the Learning Modality Inventory for Math Students, rank order your learning modality score by putting 1, 2 or 3 in the space below. Number one is for the learning preference that is most like you. If you have a tie, pick the preference you feel is most accurate.

Auditory _____

Visual _____

Kinesthetic _____

Modality learning preferences are neither good nor bad. They are concerned with how you best take in information. Depending on the subject, professors teach in various ways. In the case of mathematics, most math instructors are visual learners, and they tend to teach the way they learn best. Most of these instructors will write on the board or use a PowerPoint presentation to help you learn math.

Using Your Learning Preference to Improve Memory

There are many different techniques that can help you store information in your long-term memory and reasoning. Using your learning sense or learning preference and decreasing distraction while studying are very efficient ways to learn. Using your best learning sense (what educators call your "predominate learning modality") improves how well you learn and enhances the transfer of knowledge into long-term memory/reasoning. As you'll remember, the learning senses are vision, hearing, touching, etc. Ask yourself if you learn best by watching (vision), listening (hearing), or touching (feeling).

Another helpful tool is the Learning Preferences Modality Inventory for Math Students, available in Appendix B. It is the only learning preference inventory that has specific modality math learning preference information. This means the inventory suggests specific ways you prefer to learn math. Based on your preferred learning preference, practice those learning suggestions first. Preferences are based on genetics and environment, not ability or intelligence.

The next few sections in the textbook cover the three major types of learners and provide specific tips on how each type can streamline the memory process. You can decide if you are a social, individual or group learner. Find the section that best suits your particular needs and progress accordingly. In the meantime, here is a quick refresher on five types of learners:

- *Visual Numeric Learners* prefer to learn by reading and writing.
- *Auditory Numeric Learners* prefer to learn through lectures and other verbal communication.
- *Tactile Concrete Learners* prefer to learn through hands-on learning.
- *Social Individual Learners* prefer to learn either by themselves or by one-on-one tutoring.
- *Social Group Learners* prefer to take part in group learning.

Multiple Senses

If you have difficulty learning material from one sense, try learning material through two or three senses. Involving two or more senses improves your learning and remembering. Review the figures in this section on using your learning preferences. Whenever possible, combine learning preferences. If your primary sense is visual, and your secondary sense is auditory, write down equations while saying them out loud. Writing and reciting the material at the same time combines visual, auditory, and some tactile/concrete preferences of learning. Likewise, studying with a pen or highlighter is a visual as well as a tactile/concrete way to improve your concentration. Placing the pen or highlighter in your hand forces you to concentrate on what you are reading. After you write and recite the material back to yourself, do it five or ten more times to over-learn it.

Improving Memory for Visual and Auditory Learners

Most college students are either visual or auditory learners. While it is easier to find math teachers and tutors to accommodate these learning preferences than it is for other methods, students who learn this way should still learn to maximize their chances of success. With that in mind, read the section on this page that is specific to the way you prefer to learn and then take a look at the adjoining chart (printed on the next page). These charts present easy-to-implement strategies that are custom designed to help specific types of learners improve their success in math.

Visual (Watching) Learner

Visual learners—also known as Visual Numerical Learners—study best by repeatedly reading and writing down material. These learners get more out of reading a textbook and watching their professors write on the board than they do listening to lectures.

A visual way to decrease distractions is by using the "my mind is full" concept. Imagine that your mind is completely filled with thoughts of learning math, and other distracting thoughts cannot enter. Your mind has one-way input and output, which only responds to thinking about math when you are doing homework or studying.

Auditory (Hearing) Learner

If you are an auditory learner—one who learns best by hearing the information—then learning formulas is best accomplished by repeating them back to yourself, or recording and listening to them. In-class and Web-based lectures are perfectly suited to your preference, which gives you plenty of options.

Reading out loud is one of the best auditory ways to get important information into long-term memory. Stating facts and ideas out loud improves your ability to think and remember. If you cannot recite out loud, recite the material to yourself, emphasizing the key words.

An auditory way to improve your concentration is by becoming aware of your distractions and telling yourself to concentrate. If you are in a location where talking out loud will cause a disturbance, mouth the words "start concentrating" as you say them in your mind. This usually increases the length of time you are able to concentrate.

Visual Numeric Learner

These students learn math best by seeing it written. If you are a visual numerical learner, you may learn best by following these suggestions:

1. Use worksheets, workbooks, handouts, additional math texts and any other additional written materials.

2. Play games with, and get involved in activities with, visual printed materials such as multiplication or algebra flash cards.

3. Use visually orientated computer programs, homework programs, math websites, and phone applications like those mentioned in this text.

4. Watch YouTube videos on learning math.

5. Rework your notes using the suggestions in this text.

6. Make "3 X 5" note or flash cards putting the variables and numbers in different colors.

7. Use Study Stacks to develop your own virtual flash cards or use the virtual flash cards already developed (www.academicsuccess.com—Student Resources—Student Math Practice and Learning Sites.)

8. Use different colors of ink to emphasize different parts of each math formula.

9. Visualize numbers and formulas in detail.

10. Ask your tutor to show you how to do the problems instead of telling you how to do the problems.

11. Take pictures of the board with your smartphone, or use your phone to record a lecture.

12. Develop visual flash cards by taking pictures of concepts, rules or laws. Write down explanations or examples. Check the next picture, which has explanations or examples.

Auditory Numeric Learner

If you are an auditory numerical learner, you may learn best by following these suggestions:

1. Say the numbers to yourself or move your lips as you read the problems.

2. Record your class and play it back while reading your notes.

3. Read aloud any written explanations.

4. Make sure all important facts are spoken aloud with auditory repetition.

5. Read problems aloud and try solutions verbally as you talk yourself through them.

6. Record directions to difficult math problems and refer to them when solving those specific types of problems.

7. Record math laws and rules in your own words, by chapters, and listen to them every other day (auditory highlighting).

8. Use your smartphone or tablet to record a lecture.

9. Explain to the tutor how to work the math problems.

10. Explain to group members how to solve math problems.

11. Develop audio flash cards by recording concepts, rules or laws, and leave 15 seconds between statements so you can explain them. Check and see if you are correct.

12. During the test, sub-vocally talk yourself through the problems.

Improving Memory for Tactile/ Concrete Learners

A tactile/concrete learner needs to feel and touch material to learn it. Tactile concrete learners, who are also called "kinesthetic" learners, tend to learn best when they concretely manipulate information. Unfortunately, most math instructors do not use this learning sense. As a result, students who depend heavily upon feeling and touching for learning will usually have the most difficulty developing effective math learning techniques. This learning preference creates a problem with math learning because math is more abstract than concrete. Also, most math instructors are visual abstract learners and have difficulty teaching math tactilely. Ask for the math instructors and tutors who give the most practical examples and who may even "act out" the math problems.

As mentioned before, a tactile concrete learner will probably learn most efficiently by hands-on learning. Also, learning is most effective when physical involvement with manipulation is combined with sight and sound.

Based on the Learning Modality Inventory for Math Students, tactile concrete learners best learn math by manipulating the information that is to be taught. If you are a tactile concrete learner, you may learn best by following the suggestions in the figure printed on the next page. Try as many of these suggestions as possible and select and practice the best suggestions that help. If you do not have these manipulatives or don't know how to use them, ask the math lab supervisor or instructor if they have any manipulative materials or models. If your math lab does not have any manipulative materials, ask for help to develop your own.

Tactile/concrete learners can also use graphing calculators to improve their learning. Entering keystrokes makes it easier to remember how to solve the problems. This is also an excellent way to remember how to solve a problem when using a calculator during a test. Another way tactile/concrete learners can learn is to trace the graph with their fingers when it appears on the calculator. They should say and trace every equation to "feel" how the graph changes when using different equations.

A tactile/concrete way to improve your study concentration is by counting the number of distractions for each study session. Place a sheet of paper by your book when doing homework.

When you catch yourself not concentrating put the letter "C" on the sheet of paper. This will remind you to concentrate and get back to work. After each study period, count up the number of "C's" and watch the number decrease.

Tactile/Concrete Learner

These students learn math best by hands on learning. If you are a tactile concrete learner, you may learn best by following these suggestions:

1. Cut up a paper plate to represent a fraction of a whole.

2. Fold up a piece of paper several times and cut along the fold marks to represent a fraction of a whole.

3. In order to understand math concepts, ask to be shown how to use Cuesinaire or algebra titles as manipulatives.

4. Try to use your hands and body to "act out" a solution. For example, you may "become" the car in a rate-and-distance word problem.

5. Obtain diagrams, objects or manipulatives and incorporate activities such as drawing and writing into your study time. You may also enhance your learning by doing some type of physical activity such as walking.

6. Find a way to physically interact with common mathematics techniques. For an example, follow the directions below.

F (a) (c)

O (a) (d)

I (b) (c)

L (b) (d)

(a + b) (c + d)

FOIL is used to remember the procedure to multiply two binomials. To use FOIL, multiply the following:

- the First terms ((a) (c))
- the Outside Terms ((a) (d))
- the Inside Terms ((b) (c))
- the Last terms ((b) (d)).

To learn FOIL, trace your finger along the FOIL route.

7. Ask to use the Hands-On-Equations Learning System using manipulatives to learn basic algebra. You can go to their website (www.borenson.com) to learn more about this system and other systems to help you learn math.

8. Go to one of the "learning stores," usually in your local mall, to see if they sell manipulatives. You can also try a K-12 learning resource center to see if they have manipulatives, such as magnetic boards, that you can put letters and numbers on and move around. Also, talk to the coordinator of students with disabilities to see if they use manipulatives when tutoring their students with learning disabilities.

9. Tear up a piece of paper into several pieces and put an x on some of the pieces. Mark the other pieces with numbers 0 to 9. The pieces with the x can represent the variable and the other pieces can represent the numbers. You can now use the pieces of paper to set up and solve equations.

10. Use the virtual manipulative websites at www.academicsuccess.com — Student Resource website or Google "college math manipulative."

Activity 6.2 Use Your Learning Preference to Improve Your Math Knowledge

Now that you know your preferred learning preference, it is time to put it to use. Use the question-naireprinted below to figure out how to choose the resources that best fit your best way of learning.

1. Rank order your preferred learning preference 1-3.

Auditory   _____
Visual   _____
Kinesthetic   _____

2. Think back to the last math course you completed. How did you study for this class? Did your approach follow your best learning preference? Or did you adapt to the way your professor taught the course?

_____

_____

_____

_____.

3. The best way to use your learning preference is to use your top two learning preferences at the same time to learn material. List three learning strategies that can combine your best learning preferences:

     a.

     b.

     c.

4. Based on this learning preference, what type of professor should you seek out? Keep in mind how this professor may or may not teach his or her classes.

_____

_____

_____

_____.

General Memory Techniques

Now that you know how to use your best learning preference to improve your memory, it is time to learn a few techniques that help you remember specific information. These techniques are especially helpful when studying for tests.

A Good Study/Math Attitude

Having a positive attitude about studying will help you concentrate and improve your retention. This means you need to have at least a neutral math attitude (you neither like nor dislike it), and you should reserve the right to actually learn to like math. View studying as an opportunity to learn rather than as an unpleasant task. Tell yourself that you can learn the material and that learning it will help you pass the course and graduate.

Be a Selective Learner

Being selective in your math learning will improve your memory. Prioritize the materials you are studying. Decide which facts you need to know and which ones you can ignore. Narrow down information into laws and principles that can be generalized. Learn the laws and principles 100 percent.

Also, you must learn the math vocabulary in each chapter to continue to understand the instructor and math material.

Example: If you have been given a list of math principles and laws to learn for a test, put each one on an index card. As you go through them, create two piles: an "I already know this" pile and an "I don't know this" pile. Then, study only the "I don't know this" pile until it is completely memorized and understood.

Become an Organizer

Organizing math material into idea/fact clusters helps you learn and memorize it. Grouping similar material in a problem or calculator log are examples of categorizing information. Do not learn isolated facts; always connect them to other similar material.

Use Visual Imagery

Using mental pictures or diagrams is especially helpful for visual learners and those who are right-hemisphere dominant. Mental pictures and diagrams involve 100 percent of your brainpower. Picture the steps to solve difficult math problems in your mind.

Example: Use the Foil Method to visually learn how to multiply binomials. Memorize the face until you can sketch it from memory. During a test, you can then sketch the face onto your scratch paper and refer to it.

Make Associations

Association learning can help you remember better. Find a link between new facts and some well-established old facts and study them together. The recalling of old facts will help you remember the new ones and strengthen a mental connection between the two. Make up your own associations to remember math properties and laws.

Example: When learning the commutative property, remember that the word "commutative" sounds like the word "community." A community is made up of different types of people who could be labeled as an "a" group and a "b" group. However, in a community of "a" people and "b" people, it does not matter if we count the "a" people first or the "b" people first; we still have the same total number of people in the community. Thus, a+b=b+a. When learning the distributive law of multiplication over addition, such as a(b+c), remember that "distributive" sounds like "distributor," which is associated with giving out a product. The distributor "a" is giving its products to "b" and "c.

Use Mnemonic Devices

The use of mnemonic devices is another way to help you remember. Mnemonic devices are easily remembered words, phrases or rhymes associated with difficult-to-remember principles or facts. Chances are you've used these devices since elementary school.

Example: A mnemonic device to remember the Order of Operations is "Please Excuse My Dear Aunt Sally." The first letter in each of the words represents the math function to be completed from the first to the last. Thus, the Order of Operations is Parentheses (Please), Exponents (Excuse), Multiplication (My), Division (Dear), Addition (Aunt), and Subtraction (Sally).

Using mnemonic devices can improve a student's mathematics learning. Students making up their own mnemonic devices can remember them better than the ones given to them. Try to make up your own mnemonic device, but if you have difficulty, use the mathematic mnemonic devices on the Winning at Math Student Resource website.

Use Acronyms

Acronyms are another memory device to help you learn math. Acronyms are word forms created from the first letters of a series of words. Using acronyms improves a student's mathematics learning. Making up your own acronym devices is the best way to remember them. If you are having difficulty making up acronyms then use the Winning at Math Student Resource website.

Example: FOIL is a common math acronym. FOIL is used to remember the procedure to multiply two binomials. Each letter in the word FOIL represents a math operation. FOIL stands for First, Outside, Inside and Last, as it applies to multiplying two binomials such as (2x+3)(x+7). The First product is 2x (in the first expression) and x (in the second expression). The Outside product is 2x (in the first expression) and 7 (in the second expression). The Inside product is 3 (in the first expression) and x (in the second expression). The Last product is 3 (in the first expression) and 7 (in the second expression). This results in F ((2x)(x)) + O ((2x)(7)) + I ((3)(x)) + L ((3)(7)). Do the multiplication to get $2x^2 + 14x + 3x + 21$, which adds up to $2x^2 + 17x + 21$.

How to Use Number Sense

Number sense is a lot like common sense. It is the ability to see if your answer makes sense without using algorithms. (Algorithms are the sequential math steps used to solve problems.) An example of using number sense or estimating is in "rounding off."

Taking the time to estimate the answer to a math problem is a good way to check your answer.

Example: Solve 48 + 48 by rounding off. Rounding off means mentally changing the number (up or down) to make it more manageable to you, without using algorithms. By rounding off, 48 becomes 50 (easier to work with). 50 + 50 = 100. If the choices for answers were 104, 100, 98 and 96, you would then subtract four from the 100 (since each number was rounded up by 2) and you get 96.

Another way to use number sense is to check your answer to see if it is reasonable. Many students forget this important step and get the answer wrong. This is especially true of word or story problems.

Examples: When solving a rate-and-distance problem, use your common sense to realize that one car cannot go 500 miles per hour to catch the other car. However, the car could go 50 miles per hour.

The same common-sense rule applies to age-word problems where the age of a person cannot be 150 years but could be 15.

Further, in solving equations, x is usually a number that is less than 20. When you solve a problem for x and get 50, then this isn't reasonable, and you should re-check your calculations.

Also remember, when dealing with an equation, to make sure that you put the answer back into the equation to see if one side of the equation equals the other. If the two sides are not equal, you have the wrong answer.

If you have extra time left over after you have completed a test, you should check answers using this method. Always use all of your alloted test time.

Metacognition— Putting It All Together

Metacognition is a concept we already discussed that looks at what students are thinking when solving math problems. Using your memory process to learn how to solve math problems is the first step, but you must also be able to apply concepts to solve homework or test problems. The key to your success is the self-monitoring of problem solving, not memorizing how to do the problems. Memorization of steps instead of understanding the rules and principles leads to passive learning and unsuccessful problem solving. It is important that you develop a reliable method. Gray (1991) in her article, "Ideas in Practice: Metacognition and Mathematical Problem Solving," suggests a math solving model based on metacognition. This model of plan, monitor and evaluate is a framework for solving math problems also supported by other researchers.

Planning consists of understanding what the problem wants, the strategies to solve the problem and potential obstacles. It also includes understanding what information is required, doing the calculations and predicting the outcome.

Monitoring is putting the steps in order, keeping one's place, identifying and finding errors, understanding when additional information is needed, knowing when to use another strategy and knowing when you have part of the answer.

Evaluating includes knowing if the answer seems right (number sense), putting the answer back into the equation, doing the opposite of the function to see if the answer is correct, and measuring the efficiency of the plan and monitoring.

Using metacognition to solve math problems increases your homework and test-taking success.

For review, see Chapter Four (How to Improve Your Homework Techniques), as well as Chapter Five (Managing Anxiety and Taking Math Tests).

Activity 6.3 Developing Your Memory Techniques

Now that you have learned about different memory techniques to help you remember math information, you can develop your own. Follow the instructions below to develop different techniques.

1. Describe how you would use a good study/math attitude to improve learning.

2. Give an example of a formula you need to learn and how you would use visual imagery to learn it (cannot use book example)

3. Give an example of a math concept you are now learning and how you would use a mnemonic device or acronym to remember it (cannot use book example).

4. Explain number sense and give an example of how you would use it during homework and on a test.

   Number sense is:

   Two examples are:

Creating an Individual College Success Plan for Math

In order to make the best grades in your high school or college math courses, you need to develop a detailed plan for every semester. This plan must include a list of goals, and the steps and resources required to meet these goals. This book is designed to help you produce a plan that meets all of these requirements and more.

To illustrate what your finished plan might look like, we've printed a completed copy of the form after this section. Notice that the student who filled out this form has written her goals in a clear, concise fashion. As you can see, to properly complete this plan, you first need to determine your best learning preference. Next, you need to set your goals for your current math course(s). Finally, figure out what study strategies are best suited to your specific learning preference, then list those strategies that address your semester goals.

To fill out your My Math Success Plan, see the blank form in Appendix C.

Why This Success Plan Is Necessary

Creating a math success plan for every semester is important for many reasons.

Here are just a few of them:

- *Plans breed confidence.* Feeling prepared for a test or a class gives you the confidence you need to succeed.

- *It lets your professors know you are serious.* By filling out a math success plan, it lets your professors know you are making their class a priority.

- *It helps you figure out what does and doesn't work.* Making a success plan allows you to take stock in what study skills actually work for you.

Sections A and B

Section A is fairly straightforward. Simply list your name and year in college. List your current math course in Section B, and you are ready to move on!

Section C: Learning Information

Section C compiles everything you've worked on in this chapter—specifically your MSSE scores, your areas for improvement and your personal learning preference.

Section D

Section D is where you should write down your semester goals. You may need a second meeting with your counselor to establish the rest of your goals. Remember, these goals should relate to your expected grades, study skills improvement, study schedule and, if applicable, services offered by the disability support service office.

These goals should include the following:

1. Your overall GPA

2. The grade for your math class

3. How to improve math study skills weaknesses from the Math Study Skills Evaluation

4. Deciding how many hours a week to study math

5. Deciding which days to study math

6. How many tutoring hours a week

7. How many times you will visit your instructor

8. To review each returned test with a tutor or instructor

Section E

Section E is perhaps the most important section of this activity. It is where you put together everything you have learned in this book. If you need to work on your note-taking skills, use this space to write down your intention to use the "Seven Steps to Math Note-Taking." If you need to work on your test-taking skills, write down what you have learned in Chapter 5.

What you write should be completely personalized. No two students share the exact same strengths and weaknesses. Be truthful and accurate. As you complete this section, remember that you do not need to go into too much detail. Just write down the exact strategies you are going to use from this text,

and make sure you remember where to find them. In fact, it is a good idea to write down page numbers next to each strategy.

Section F

Section F is where you log all of the motivational strategies you have learned about in this chapter. For example, if you have a problem with procrastination, you would write something like, "I will figure out the reasons for my procrastination and overcome them." This is also where you list the positive statements you have created to replace any negative talk.

Completing Your Plan

If you need help finishing your plan, visit any or all of the following:

- *an advisor/counselor*

- *a favorite instructor*

- *a math instructor*

- *a veteran's adviser*

- *a disability adviser*

All of these professionals are able to give useful advice on a wide range of subjects. Also keep in mind that you should revist this plan every time you take a test. If you do not make the grade you want, you might need to revise your plan. Seek help from your instructor in making these revisions. Ask for additional suggestions. If you *did* make the grade you wanted, you should share this information with the anyone with whom you have discussed your plan. Anyone who has helped you complete your plan deserves feedback, as it can reinforce efforts to devise and use effective strategies.

In the end, you will be glad to have completed your math success plan. It will keep you on task for the semester and help reduce your test anxiety (see example on the next page). If you are a student with a disability or a veteran and need extra help, refer to the student workbook *My Math Success Plan* (Nolting 2012).

My Math Success Plan (Example)

Semester: Fall 2019

A: Student Information
>   Name: Sally Student
>   Year in College: Sophomore

B: Course: Intermediate Algebra

C: Learning Information

I am predominately a visual learner.

Based on my MSSE scores, I need to work on note-taking and homework techniques.

D: Semester Goals

1. I will obtain a 3.0 GPA.
2. I will make a "B" in elementary algebra/algebra II.
3. I will improve my math study skills weaknesses by working on the suggestions from the computerized Math Study Skills Evaluation.
4. I will set up a study schedule and each week will complete a study-goals sheet.
5. I will attend tutorial sessions.
6. I will see my math instructor every two weeks and after each major test.

E: Math Study Strategies

Use math note-taking system
Color code notes
Develop a math glossary
Use online homework system
Learn relaxation techniques
Develop my own test-taking system

F: Motivation Strategies

1. I will make an appointment with my math teacher.
2. I will reward myself when completing a short-term goal.
3. I will learn the reasons for my procrastination and overcome them.
4. I will tell myself positive statements everyday.
5. I will tell myself by passing math, I will get my business degree.

Chapter Six: Checklist for Knowledge and Behaviors

Put a check after understanding the knowledge statements and fill in the behavioral activities.

Chapter Knowledge

1. I know that improving my affective characteristics (such as motivation and study skills) will improve my math learning and grades. _____

2. I know that it is very important to have enough working memory to recall information from long-term memory to solve a problem. _____

3. I know that transforming working memory into long-term memory is the major memory problem for most students. _____

4. I know that while studying, many students do not complete this memory-shifting process. _____

5. I know that understanding the stages of memory and using memory techniques can help me learn math. _____

6. I understand that using my best learning modality can improve my memory. _____

7. I understand that by combining two of my best learning modalities it can greatly enhance my memory. _____

8. I understand that common memory techniques include maintaining a good math/study attitude, becoming a selective learner, becoming an organizer, using visual imagery, making associations, using mnemonic devices and acronyms. _____

9. I used the metacognition model of planning, monitoring, and evaluating to improve my math success. _____

10. I completed My Math Success Plan. ____

11. Based on My Math Success Plan, I know which math success strategies to improve. _____

Behavioral Activities

1. I reviewed the Stages of Memory and understand each stage and how the stages interact. ___

2. I reviewed the Stages of Memory and know the common problems associated with each stage and how to overcome them. ___

3. My best learning modality is _____ and I discussed with my tutor how to best to tutor me based on my preference on this date / / .

4. I talked to my classmates about their learning preferences to discover strategies. _____

5. I shared My Math Success Plan with my counselor, instructor, or tutor and discussed how to improve math success. ____

Name: _____　　Date: _____

Assignment for Chapter 6

On a separate sheet of paper, answer the following questions:

1. How does quality of instruction affect your math grades?

2. How do affective characteristics affect your grades?

3. Draw the Stages of Memory and list which stage is your strength and which one you need to improve, as well as the reasons why.

4. List and describe the three different types of learning modality preferences?

5. List your best modality learning preference and describe five different strategies from that preference to improve learning.

6. How does your learning preference match up with your current professor's? If there is a mismatch, what can you do?

7. List two general memory techniques and describe how you use them to remember math formulas or concepts.

8. List and describe three reasons for developing your math success plan.

9. Describe strengths and areas to improve on in your "My Math Success Plan".

10. List five strategies that you will implement this week to improve your "My Math Success Plan."

APPENDIX

Apps, Websites, and Search Engines for Academic Support

The apps and websites below are resources to improving learning. Some of the apps are for recording information and other apps and Web sites are for learning math and checking homework problems. Review these resources to discover which one are best for you.

Recording Apps

1. Smart Voice Recorder – Recorder and label recording

2. Evernote – Type in notes, take photo of notes, record notes, attach a file, hand write and sync with computer.

3. Voice Recorder - can record information on your smart phone.

4. Photos - Can show photos of problems from the board or any written material to your tutor or instructor.

5. Video Recorded - Can video record lectures or tutoring.

Learning Math and Checking Answers

1. My Script Calculator – can write in arithmetic problems and solve them.

2. Algebra Tutor- solves arithmetic and algebra problems and has practice problems.

3. Algeo – multiply, Squares, sin, cos graphing solutions, and f(x).

4. Photomath – take pictures of equations and solves them on your phone.

5. Web Math Algebra - https://tinyurl.com/c4bo7gf - This is a free site to help solve algebra problem. Also go to the bottom of the page to see similar apps for high school and college.

6. Wolfram Algebra app - http://products.wolframalpha.com/courseassistants/algebra.html - Algebra course assistant for high school and college and the App cost of $1.99.

7. Sonocent – records lectures and turns audio into visual blocks. It also allows for colored highlighting, and combines photos and text notes.

8. Purple Math - www.Purplemath.com - One of the oldest sites for all levels of algebra.

9. Khan academy - www.khanaccademy.com - This site has videos on solving all levels of math problems and you can select the concept to be learned.

10. You Tube - www.YouTube.com - This site has videos on doing all levels of math problems. Type in the level of math such as Intermediate Algebra or the concept such as factoring trinomials.

11. Google and Bing – These search engines can be used to find examples and lectures. Just put in mathematical phrases such as "solving quadratic equations" and a list of sites will appear.

Learning Modality Inventory for Math Students

The following survey can help you discover how you best learn math. Answer the questions based on what you are like. There are no right or wrong answers. The more you answer truthfully, the more you will be able to use the results to improve studying math. "1" means the statement is hardly like you. "4" means the statement is really like you. Then, if you think the statement is somewhere in between, decide if it is a "2" or a "3."

Questions

	Least like me		Most like me	
1. Reading a math problem out loud helps me learn better when I am studying.	1	2	3	4
2. I learn math better if I can talk about it.	1	2	3	4
3. I select certain problems and memorize what they look like so I can use them to help me remember on a math test.	1	2	3	4
4. Making things with my hands helps me learn better.	1	2	3	4
5. Drawing a picture of the word problem helps me understand how to do it on a test.	1	2	3	4
6. Math makes more sense when I see it worked out on the board.	1	2	3	4
7. Moving around while studying helps me concentrate and learn more.	1	2	3	4
8. I understand written instructions better than ones told to me.	1	2	3	4
9. I memorize what a problem looks like so I can remember it better on a test or quiz.	1	2	3	4

Questions	Least like me			Most like me
10. I repeat steps to a problem out loud or to myself in order to remember what I am supposed to do.	1	2	3	4
11. Watching someone complete a math problem helps me understand more than listening to someone tell me how to do it.	1	2	3	4
12. Talking about a math problem while learning in class helps me understand it better.	1	2	3	4
13. I learn math better when I watch someone do it.	1	2	3	4
14. When I take a test, I read the problems to myself softly.	1	2	3	4
15. When I solve a math problem on a test, I picture my notes in my head to help me remember how to solve it.	1	2	3	4
16. I enjoy making things with my hands for a hobby.	1	2	3	4
17. Math makes more sense when someone talks about it while doing it on the board rather than just doing it on the board.	1	2	3	4
18. Explaining a math problem to someone else helps me learn better when I am studying.	1	2	3	4
19. Looking at a picture from my notes or math book helps me understand a math problem.	1	2	3	4
20. Making study aids with my hands helps me learn better.	1	2	3	4
21. I understand instructions better when someone tells me what they are.	1	2	3	4
22. I memorize sentences or words I can say to myself to help me remember how to do problems on a test.	1	2	3	4
23. Pictures and charts help me see how all the parts of a word problem work together.	1	2	3	4
24. I enjoy putting things together.	1	2	3	4
25. When I solve a problem on a math test, I talk my way through it in my head or softly to myself.	1	2	3	4

Scoring Your Results

Step One: Fill in each answer score in the appropriate question number. Add the column totals. Divide Column Totals A and B by 2. Those numbers will be your final column totals. Leave Column C total as is.

Column A	Column B	Column C
1. _____	3. _____	4. _____
2. _____	5. _____	7. _____
10. _____	6. _____	16. _____
12. _____	8. _____	20. _____
14. _____	9. _____	24. _____
17. _____	11. _____	
18. _____	13. _____	
21. _____	15. _____	
22. _____	19. _____	
25. _____	23. _____	
A total _____ /2 =_____ Column	B total _____ /2 =_____ Column Total	C Total _____ (Do not divide).

Step Two: Fill in the number of squares to represent each column total. Any total greater than 12 indicates that modality style as a strength when you learn math. You can be strong in more than one modality. If none of the totals equal 12 squares, your highest score is your strongest modality. If you have a tie, pick the first one that comes to mind as your strongest.

	Least Like Me																		Most Like Me
Modality	1			5				10				15				20
A = Auditory																
B = Visual																
C = Kinesthetic																

APPENDIX

My Math Success Plan

Semester:

A: Student Information
Name:
Year in College:

B: Course

C: Learning Information

D: Semester Goals

1.

2.

3.

4.

5.

6.

E: Math Study Strategies

F: Motivation Strategies

Classroom Group Learning Activities

This appendix helps improve study skills by offering suggestions for classroom group activities. Integrate these activities as part of a lecture for the entire classroom, as part of small student group sessions, or as a combination of both. Below are group activities for each chapter. Instructors can select group activities best suited for students and desired learning outcomes. Instructors can also reword group activities to best suit their classroom and to address time constraints. (The *Winning at Math* teacher's manual will have additional information on how to conduct group activities).

Chapter 1: How Learning Math is Different and How to Take Control of Your Learning

1. *Classroom Lecture* — Students attending math classes have all types of attitudes toward math. How do you like math? Do you know that the more math you take, the more money you make?

2. *Student Group* — How is learning math in college different from high school? How is learning math different from other college courses (except STEM courses)?

3. *Classroom Lecture and Student Group* — All of you have taken the Math Study Skills Evaluation and have access to your results. From a sample evaluation, we will, as a group, interpret what these results mean. Remember, a low score means that you have a greater chance to improve success. Now, discuss your results with the student next to you. What are your strengths, and what areas do you need to improve? Go ahead and read the information in the *Winning at Math* text before we discuss it in class.

4. *Student Group* — Many students have trouble believing they can be successful in math. Students need to develop math self-efficacy and mindset concepts. Among yourselves, discuss how you can accomplish this; then, each group should share ideas with other groups.

Chapter 2: How to Improve Listening and Note-Taking Skills

1. *Classroom Lecture* — From the review of an example student's notes, it appears a note-taking system is needed. The instructor describes the "Seven Steps to Taking Notes," then draws the three-column note-taking design on the board. Students draw the system in their notebooks, and the instructor demonstrates using the system to solve a problem. Students participate in the lecture by telling the instructor key words and explanations for steps. At the end of class, students compare notes to fill in gaps.

2. *Student Group* — Students are asked to take notes in class. The last five minutes of class, they share and discuss these notes. Meanwhile, the instructor goes around the classroom and observes and comments on what he or she finds.

3. *Instructor and Student Group* — Many types of technology exist to help improve note-taking and learning. This includes apps and photos. The instructor reviews

note-taking technology at home and shows examples in class. In groups, students discuss their favorite note-taking technology (including apps). Then, the instructor describes how to best use this technology in class, as well as when to take pictures of problems.

Chapter 3: How to Improve Study Environment, Time-Management, and Reading

1. *Student Group* — When it comes to learning and studying, students have different locations and strategies that best work for them. Few, however, share this information with other students. In small groups, students should discuss where they study, when they study different subjects, how much they study for math and other subjects, and, finally, their overall study plans. Meanwhile, the instructor walks around the room, listening.

2. *Instructor* — Many students claim they do not have enough time to study; however, most do not know how much time they actually spend doing so (especially for math classes). Studying math includes homework, reviewing, and preparing for tests. We are now going to complete a study schedule, which will include how many hours you commit to studying math, the best time to study math, and the grade you want.

3. *Instructor and Student Group* — Instructors have long asked students to read their standard or online textbooks; however, almost all students do not have a textbook reading strategy. This is one reason students do not value reading their texts. In this activity, the instructor selects a textbook section and leads students in practicing the "Ten Steps to Better Understanding What You Read." Students then develop their own personal reading steps, which consist of at least five steps. They then share these steps with a group.

Chapter 4: How to Improve Your Homework Techniques

1. *Student Group* — Many students do not know the reasons for doing math homework, how other students complete their math homework, homework strategies, or the best time to complete homework. Students should discuss these issues in small groups. During this activity, the instructor walks around the room listening to students.

2. *Instructor and Student Group* — Though instructors frequently stress the importance of homework in test preparation, few students have an ironclad homework strategy. This is why many complete their homework and still fail tests. In this activity, the instructor selects a homework section or develops practice homework problems and leads the students in practicing the "Ten Steps to Doing Your Math Homework." Afterward, students develop their own personal homework steps, which consist of at least five steps. Students then share these personalized steps with the class.

3. *Student Group* — Many students have difficulty learning math concepts while in the classroom or doing homework. Students now depend more and more on tutoring and classmates for help—to the point of developing in-person or online study groups. Many, however, do not know how to best use a tutor and get help from classmates. In small groups, students should discuss how to be an effective tutoree and how and when they should seek help from their peers. After the discussion, the instructor should provide his or her own thoughts on these issues.

Chapter 5: Math Anxiety and Taking Math Tests

1. *Student Group* — Many students have math anxiety and math test anxiety. These anxieties come from different experiences and times in their lives. Some students do not have these anxieties but may have them in the future. In small groups, students should discuss anxiety issues and where they come from.

2. *Instructors* — Students have different types of test anxiety. In this activity, the instructor discusses the difference between emotional and worry anxiety and how these anxieties affect learning and taking tests. The instructor then leads students in practicing short-term relaxation techniques. Student then select their best short-term relaxation techniques to use during tests.

3. *Instructor and Student Group* — Many students have been taught how to take multiple-choice tests; few, however, have been taught how to take math tests. In this activity, the instructor reviews the "Ten Test-Taking Techniques for Classroom or Computer-Based Testing." Students then develop their own personal test-taking steps, which consist of at least five steps. They then share these steps with a group.

4. *Instructor* — Students need feedback on the results of their tests. This will keep them from making the same types of errors. However, many students have not been taught how to effectively assess test-taking errors. In this activity, the instructor returns tests to students and goes through the "Six Types of Test-Taking Errors." Students then record the number of points lost for each type of error. On the next test, students will then be aware of errors, so they will not repeat past mistakes.

Chapter 6: Assessing and Using Your Memory and Math Learning Strategies

1. *Instructor and Student Group* — Most students are not aware of the learning process. Many think that doing more homework is the solution to all learning problems. Doing more homework may be *a* solution; however, in many cases, it is not the *only* solution to improve learning. In this activity, the instructor reviews the stages of memory and how each stage affects learning. The instructor then assigns each student group one of the student scenarios to review. The groups then review the scenario to determine the learning strength, learning areas to improve, and solution that are not described in the text. Groups then share these finding with other groups.

2. *Student Group* — Students have different preferences toward how they learn material. Their modality preferences involve how they best input information into their brains. In this activity, the instructor has students take the *Learning Modality Inventory for Math Students* either before or during class. Students then discuss their learning preference with their group, as well as the different types of visual, auditory, or tactical/concrete learning strategies they are or could be using. Each student then records the learning strategies from their two best learning preferences. These are their best strategies to learn math.

3. *Instructor and Student Group* — Students usually try to improve their math success by merely studying harder without an overall plan. Students who develop math success plans know what strategies to best use, as well as whether these strategies work or need to be changed. In this activity, the instructor discusses how to develop an *Individual College Success Plan for Math*. With their groups, students then develop their success plans based on the template in the text. They then share their plans and give a copy to their instructor. After each test, students review this plan.

Bibliography

Acee, T., Biggs, T., Holschuk, B., Daniels, S & Schrauth, M (2017). "Student perceived interference to college and math Success." Journal of Developmental Education, 40, (2), 1-9.

Ashcraft, M & Kirk, E. (2001). "The relationships among working memory, math anxiety, and performance." *Journal of Experimental Psychology*: General, 130 (2), 224-237.

Bandura, A. (1982). "The psychology of chance encounters and life paths." *American Psychologist*, 37, 747-755.

Boaler, J. (2016). Mathematical Mindsets. Josse-Bass. San Franciso, CA.

Bloom, B. (1976). *Human Characteristics and School Learning*. New York: McGraw-Hill Book Company. (p. 35)

Boylan, H. (2011) "Improving Success in Developmental Mathematics: An Interview with Paul Nolting." Journal(of(Developmental (Education, Volume 34, Issue 3, Spring 2011.

Brunye, T., Mahoney, C., Giles, G., Rapp, D. Taylor, H., & Kanarek, R. (2013). "Learning to relax: Evaluating four brief interventions for overcoming the negative emotions accompanying math anxiety." *Learning and Individual Differences*, 27, 1-7.

Butler, P. (1981). *Talking to Yourself. Learning the Language of Self-Report.* San Francisco: Harper & Row. (p. 219)

Deweck, C. (2016). Mindset: The new psychology of success. New York, Ballantine Books.

Farr, M & Ludden (2013) *Best Jobs for the 21st Century*. Indianapolis, IN: JIST Works pp 84-87 (p. 25)

Foley, A., Herts, J., Brogonovi, F., Guerriero, S., Levine, S., & Beilock, S. (2017). "The Math Anxeity-Performance Link: A Global Phenomenon." *Association for Psychological Science*, 26 (1) 52- 58.

Gray, S. (1991). "Ideas in Practice: Metacognition and Mathematical Problem Solving," *Journal of Developmental Education*, 14 (3), 24 - 30.

Nolting, K. (2008). *Learning Modality Inventory for Math Students*. Bradenton, FL: Academic Success Press, Inc. (p. 46)

Nolting, P. (1987). *How to Reduce Test Anxiety, a CD*. Bradenton, FL: Academic Success Press, Inc. (p.40)

Nolting, P. D. (2014). *My Math Success Plan*. Bradenton, FL: Academic Success Press, Inc. (p. 40)

Nolting, P. (2012). Web-Based Test Anxiety Reduction Program w/Manual and Audio Flies. Bradenton, FL :Academic Success Press, Inc.

Richardson. F, and Suinn, R. (1973). "A comparison of traditional systematic desensitization , accelerated mass desensitization, and mathematics anxiety." Behavior Therapy . No. 4, pp. 212-218. (p. 57)

Scheier, M. & Carver, C (1985). "The Phycology of Optimism and Pessimism: Theories of Research and Findings." Positive Psychology. Org.uk.

Schunk, D. H. (1991). "Self-efficacy and academic motivation," *Educational Psychologist*, 26, 207-231.

Spielberger, C. (1980). *Test Attitude Inventory*. Redwood, California: Mind Garden.

Tobias, S (1978). "Who's Afraid of Math and Why?" *Atlantic Monthly*, September, pp. 63-65. (p. 57)

Wernersback, B., Ceowley, S., Batts, S., Rosenthal, C (2014)   "Study Skills Impact on Academic Self- Efficacy."   Journal of Developmental Education, 37. (3), 14 – 23.

Zientek, L. , Ozel, Z. , Fong, C., Griffin, M. (2013). "Student Success in developmental mathematics courses," *Community College Journal of Research and Practice*, 17, 990 - 1010.

Zientec, Fong & Phelps, (2017). "Sources of self-efficacy of community college students enrolled in developmental mathematics." Received 0 Sep 2016, Acceptee 24 Mar 2017, Published online: 21 Aug 2017.

About the Author

Copyright 2014 Randy Kennedy

Over the past 30 years, Dr. Paul and Kimberly Nolting have helped thousands of students improve their math learning skills and obtain better grades. They have consulted with over 100 colleges and universities. Dr. Nolting is a national expert in assessing math learning problems, developing effective student learning strategies, assessing institutional variables that affect math success, tutor training and math study skills. He is also an expert in how to help students with disabilities and Wounded Warriors become successful in math. He has been a undergraduate instructor, a graduate instructor, a learning specialist, an institutional test administrator, Student Support Services Director, Title III director, and a math lab and disability coordinator.

Dr. Nolting holds a Ph.D. in Education in Curriculum and Instruction from the University of South Florida. His dissertation was on using math study skills to improve academic achievement. His expertise ranges from designing math study skills curriculum to redesigning math courses. He is also an expert in disabilities as they relate to mathematics learning and how to set up effective accommodations. Since his dissertation in 1986 on improving math success for developmental math students with math study skills intervention, he has continued to conduct mathematics research, consult, serve as an interview subject for journal articles, write journal articles, and conduct national training.

Dr. Nolting has conducted numerous national workshops on math learning and disability issues at the American Math Association of Two Year College (AMATYC), American Mathematics Association (MAA), National Developmental Education Association (NADE), and the Association on Higher Education and Disabilities (AHEAD). He has been the keynote speaker at many state conferences. He was a consultant for the American College Test (ACT) and the Texas Higher Education Coordinating Board.

Dr. Nolting has been widely acclaimed for his ability to communicate with faculty and students on the subject of improving math learning. He now helps colleges and universities redesign math courses to meet new curriculum requirements, and also assists institutions improve retention rates. He also helps devolop Quality Enhancement Plans (QEPs), one of which one won QEP of the year, state wide mandates and improving retention. His team is currently working on a QEP that will redesign a college's developmental math curriculum to better integrate math study skills, manipulatives and tutoring. The pilot course has a 71% pass rate.

Dr. Nolting is also a nationally recognized consultant and trainer of math study skills, math faculty training, tutor/learning assistance training and improving classroom success. He was interviewed by Dr. Hunter Boylan as a national expert in the Journal of Developmental Education. The article was titled, "Improving Success In Developmental Mathematics: An Interview with Paul Nolting." He was also interviewed by U.S. News and World Report about developmental math and online math success. Finally, he coordinated two National Math Summits: the first as a pre-conference to the 2013 AMATYC national conference, and the second as a pre-conference to the 2016 NADE national conference. The summits were a response to a nationwide need for mathematics course redesigns and assessments. The summits featured panels of national experts along with workshops to help college faculty and administrators develop their own, "Math Success Plan for College Innovation." Between those summits he also coordinated math panels at the NADE, AMAYC and MAA conferences.

He has coordinated the third National Mathematical Summit: For Math in the First Two Years. This summit took place as a pre–conference to the 2018 AMATYC national conference. He conducted three workshops, as well as the beginning and ending panels. NADE signed on as co-sponsor, and additional sponsors included National Center for Developmental Education, Carnegie Foundation, Dana Center, and the MAA. This summit was the largest summit yet and featured the most national experts.

He is also well-regarded for his ability to teach faculty and tutors about learning styles. This process includes assisting administrators as they develop affective math and study.

Over the last thirty years, Dr. Nolting has consulted with over 100 colleges, universities and high school campuses, including the University of Massachusetts, Florida State University, New Jersey City University, Rucker University, University of Colorado-Bolder, Texas Tech University, Black Hills State University, Tennessee Tech University, Austin Pea University, Clemson University, Colorado State University, the University of Connecticut, Moorhead State University, and the University of Louisville.

Most recently Dr. Nolting and his wife, Kimberly, returned to the Gulf University of Science and Technology to follow up on results of their first visit and to review the implementation of math study skills into math course sections. Kimberly conducted workshops on math self-efficacy and improving advisement with counselors. Dr. Nolting also recently presented a NADE (now called National Organization for Student Success) conference workshop with math faculty on the positive results of implementing math study skills into curriculum.

Other colleges with which he has consulted include San Antonio College, St. Louis Community College, J. Sargeant Reynolds College, Montgomery College, Broward College, Miami-Dade College, Northeast State Technical Community College, Landmark College, Denver Community College, Valencia College, Mesa Community College, Glendale Community College, Austin Community College, Fresno City College, Housatonic Community College, St. Petersburg College, and Santa Barbara City College. He is now working with colleges and universities to design their math co-requisite curriculum.

He also has written seven other books, three DVDs, two CDs and authored three websites. His latest two books are *My Math Success Plan* and *Mathematics and Disability Handbook*. The latter is a workbook for wounded warriors and students with disabilities, which combines math study skills and educational information on how disabilities affect math learning. The Mathematics and Disability Handbook serves as a reference text for math instructors and disability/veteran coordinators.

Index